SOW, GROW, AND HARVEST

A YEAR-ROUND GUIDE TO GARDENING AND ARRANGING CUT FLOWERS

Translated from the German by Rachel Joerges. Originally published in German language under the title *Slowflowers – Wilde Gärten und ungezähmte Bouquets*. Copyright © 2022 Haupt, Berne, Switzerland. Photographs by Grit Hartung, Germany. Book design by Grit Hartung, Germany.

English-language edition published by
© 2025 Schiffer Publishing
Library of Congress Control Number: 2024941454

All rights reserved. No part of this work may be reproduced or used in any form or by any means—graphic, electronic, or mechanical, including photocopying or information storage and retrieval systems—without written permission from the publisher.

The scanning, uploading, and distribution of this book or any part thereof via the Internet or any other means without the permission of the publisher is illegal and punishable by law. Please purchase only authorized editions and do not participate in or encourage the electronic piracy of copyrighted materials. "Schiffer," "Schiffer Publishing, Ltd.," and the pen and inkwell logo are registered trademarks of Schiffer Publishing, Ltd.

Type set in: Gellatio/FreightTextPro
Cover design by: Danielle Farmer
ISBN: 978-0-7643-6898-1
ePub: 978-1-5073-0544-7
Printed in India

Published by Schiffer Publishing, Ltd.
4880 Lower Valley Road
Atglen, PA 19310
Phone: (610) 593-1777; Fax: (610) 593-2002
Email: info@schifferbooks.com
Web: www.schifferbooks.com

For our complete selection of fine books on this and related subjects, please visit our website at www.schifferbooks.com. You may also write for a free catalog. Schiffer Publishing's titles are available at special discounts for bulk purchases for sales promotions or premiums. Special editions, including personalized covers, corporate imprints, and excerpts, can be created in large quantities for special needs. For more information, contact the publisher.

For **Erna, Evelyn** & **Jörg, Clemens,** and **Dirk**, and for everyone who believes in the wild idea of slow, homegrown flowers.

For **Nele** and **Lill,** the most wonderful growing flowers.

All information in this book has been carefully researched, checked, and tested and reflects the current state of knowledge at the time of the book's publication. However, knowledge as well as laws regarding plant cultivation continue to develop and change, and new discoveries are added. Therefore, I would like to ask each reader to check whether the respective findings are outdated or not. This especially is relevant in regard to plant strengthening and biological fertilizers: here I recommend reading the included instructions carefully and using products accordingly. Furthermore, all of the information in this book was written in reference to German regulations, and the regulations may differ widely in different countries, so it is important to check with your local authorities: calling your government agency associated with agriculture is a good place to start.

The plant growth and flowering times are influenced by climate factors. The flowering and harvesting times given in the book are approximate values that can be transferred to your own garden's location/climate and adjusted if necessary.

SOW, GROW, AND HARVEST

A YEAR-ROUND GUIDE TO GARDENING AND ARRANGING CUT FLOWERS

Chantal Remmert

Photography by Grit Hartung

4880 Lower Valley Road · Atglen, PA 19310

Table of Contents

Foreword	6
Introduction	9

INTRODUCTION

Gardening Basics	12
Seasons, Geography, and Weather	12
Botany	14
Soil	16
Locations	18
Garden Management	20
Long-Handled Tools	22
Hand Tools	24
Vases	26
Materials	28

SPRING

Spring Essentials	32
Prepare Soil and Beds	34
Cultivation	38
Divide Perennials	42
Take Cuttings	46
Planting	48
Spring Garden DIY	52
Willow Tea	54
Spring Blooms	56
Double Daffodil	58
Apple Blossom	60
Anemone	63
Tulip	64
Buttercup	67
Spring Floral Design	68
Scented Arrangement	71

SUMMER

Summer Essentials	78
Weeding and Cleaning Out	80
Fences, Netting, and Climbing Aids	82
Fertilizing and Strengthening	85
Cutting and Harvesting	88
Summer Garden DIY	92
Nettle Liquid Manure	94
Drip Irrigation	97
Summer Blooms	100
Peony	102
Love-in-a-Mist	104
Snapdragon	107
Garden Cosmos	109
Annual Larkspur	110
Summer Floral Design	114
Tying the Bouquet	117
Wrapping the Bouquet	124

AUTUMN

Autumn Essentials	130
Collect Seeds	132
Autumn Sowing and Planting	136
Dig Up and Store Dahlias	140
Autumn Garden DIY	144
Drying Flowers	146
Autumn Blooms	148
Garden Rose	150
Dahlia	153
Panicled Hydrangea	155
Chrysanthemum	156
Autumn Floral Design	158
Dried-Flower Wreath	161

WINTER

Winter Essentials	170
Overwintering Plants	172
Planning Your Beds	176
Rose Pruning	180
Winter Garden DIY	182
Divide Dahlia Tubers	184
Build a Heating Mat	188
Winter Blooms	190
Amaryllis	192
Flowering Cabbage	195
Christmas Rose	197
Winter Floral Design	200
Festive Centerpiece	202

The Authors	208
Acknowledgments	209
Bloom and Harvest Calendar	210
Garden Work Calendar	212
Resources	214
Index	218
Note	223

Foreword

The love of flowers has been with me as far back as I can remember. After studying landscape architecture at the Technical University of Berlin, my wish to work closer with plants started to grow. In the beginning of 2016, I founded Erna Primula—Blumen Studio (or, in English, Flower Studio) in Leipzig.

I was inspired by Ingrid Carozzi's book *Brooklyn Flowers* and her company "Tin Can Studios" in Brooklyn, Erin Benzakein and her flower farm named "Floret," and Katie Davis with her company "Ponderosa and Thyme." I wanted to build a company: sustainable and environmentally friendly, regional and seasonal, and full of floral abundance.

Starting in the beginning of 2018, I began to grow my own sustainable flowers on half an acre (2,300 m²) in Leipzig. I was self-taught during this period, using reference literature, online workshops, and Instagram channels.

To be as sustainable and environmentally friendly as possible, I work in cycles. All substances and materials used are subject to close scrutiny. Cut greens and wilted flowers are composted, and chicken wire is used to support flowers and, just like the vases from the flea market, reused for years and decades to come.

Along with fresh-cut flowers, I also produce under the name "Erna Primula" my own sustainable seeds.

Meanwhile, the nursery in Leipzig has moved to the Schwäbisch Hall in Baden-Wuerttemberg.

Introduction

It's not just plants, but also hope, confidence, and joy that grow while we cultivate flowers. A small seed is placed into the earth, nourished, and cared for, and three months later the lushest bouquets can be harvested.

The work in the garden gives us the opportunity to see the results and our work directly, because whoever sows flowers will reap joy! Additionally, gardeners intensely perceive the seasons, their colors, their forms, and their smells. All this is part of a lifestyle that is now known as the slow-flowers movement. I believe in slow flowers and their ability to enrich one's life, and the philosophy of slow flowers intersperses the entirety of this book.

With the harvest we dedicate ourselves to another joyful facet of growing slow flowers: sustainable processing! For me, this means first and foremost thinking in cycles. Foam, hot-glue guns, and plastic tape turn a natural product into residual waste. That is why all materials are checked before use to see if they are reusable and able to be repurposed, recyclable, or compostable. If not, we look for another solution.

With this book, I would like to pass on my experiences with sustainable flower gardening. Techniques will be described that I have discovered or developed and verified. We are all still on a journey—no one is perfect, and it should always be our aspiration to keep improving ourselves and never stand still.

And at the end of the day, your feet should be dirty, your hair ruffled, and your eyes glowing!

—Author unknown

Introduction

Gardening Basics

SEASONS, GEOGRAPHY, AND WEATHER

Seasons

This book is split into the four seasons of spring, summer, autumn, and winter. For this, I orient myself on the meteorological calendar: spring begins on March 1 and autumn on September 1. Please note, however, that you may have to adjust my season schedule in all elements throughout this book to match the climate where you reside. Your local garden center can help you do this, as can simple queries in a search engine.

Climate and Geography

Climate describes the overall weather over many years. My examples are drawn from Germany, but again, you can adapt: and many regions in Europe, Asia, and North America (particularly the Northeast) share very similar climates for planting purposes. Leipzig is in a temperate climate zone, which is transitional between the maritime and continental climate zones. The city sits in a lowland basin and extends across natural elevations about 328–524 feet (100–160 m) above sea level.

In contrast, Allgaü, for example, lies much higher; Kempten is 3,264 feet (995 m) above sea level, which is why frost and snow occur significantly earlier in the autumn, and the frost-free temperatures start later in the spring.

Freiburg, on the other hand, is located at 912 feet (278 m) above sea level, but the vital factor here is less its location above sea level and more its geographic position. The Rhine rift valley between Basel and Karlsruhe, where Freiburg is located, is very warm, which is why the cultivation of wine is especially worthwhile. Therefore, the season start is one month earlier in the spring in Freiburg than in Leipzig, which is at a similar altitude.

In addition to the larger geographic context of the region where we garden, there are also smaller variables that influence our garden climates. For example, whether the garden is located on a north-facing slope or a south-facing slope and whether it is surrounded by shady buildings or located in a windy corridor are decisive factors for the respective microclimate. My nursery in Leipzig, for example, is open from north to south; this creates a cold air corridor in autumn and winter. It causes us to have frost on the leaves earlier than the city parks in Leipzig that are surrounded by buildings.

Weather

To plan my garden work well, the weather for the upcoming day is a decisive factor. That is why there are multiple weather apps on my smartphone that I check regularly. For example, when I plant in the spring: if rain is in the forecast, I will plant, because then the seedlings grow best! In the summer months, the temperatures decide when to start harvesting in the morning, and the amount of rainfall decides when and how much to water. And in late autumn, when the first frost is predicted, there is a royal, final harvest!

When Will There Be Frost?

The first and last frost belong to some of the most important pieces of information for the flower gardener. In Germany, much of Europe, and the northern half of the United States, some of Cananda, and some of Asia, the first frost tends to be between the beginning of October and the end of November. With it comes the end of the outdoor season because it damages all heat-loving annual plants and dahlias. After that, only a few garden roses, flowering cabbage, and chrysanthemums bloom outdoors.

But again, there are exceptions to the rule. In 2020, we surprisingly had a light frost the night of October 6–7. Normally, after the first frost, the dahlia tubers are dug up and stored. However, this first frost only lightly touched the dahlias, resulting in scattered brown spots on the plants.

According to the weather forecast, a stable high with warmer temperatures was expected over the next two weeks. Therefore, we had only cut back the dahlias and had not dug them up yet. Amazingly, this allowed us to harvest lush dahlias through the end of November, when true winter temperatures arrived.

Make sure to check with your local garden center, wherever on Earth you are located, to familiarize yourself with the regional seasons there. However, in Germany and similar climate regions, the last frost tends to occur around mid-May, on the so-called *Eisheiligen* (Ice Saints: a word we use in Germany to denote frost markers). It separates the frost-hardy annual flowers, such as love-in-a-mist and larkspur, from the frost-sensitive species; for example, garden cosmos and zinnias. Every year, on a sunny April day, I wonder if frost will really come again or not. For the most part, it tends to come back! But the *Eisheiligen* can also fail—it's rare, but it happens—that's nature! By the way, many of the frost-tolerant annual flowers can also be sown in the fall—you can read more about this on page 136.

If frost-sensitive crops have been set too early, they can be covered with fleece or a blanket at night to protect them from the cold temperatures.

It is important to be familiar with the weather, climate, and geography of your region. But don't worry: usually all it takes is a little chat with your experienced gardening neighbors, a quick internet search, and a weather app, and experience will take care of the rest.

BOTANY

Introduction

The most beautiful thing about plants is that they actually grow on their own!

In order to harvest many cut flowers from your own garden, you don't need a lot of equipment or technology. Plants' needs are simple: they need light, water, and nutrition. If plants are not growing well, their conditions probably have too much or too little of one or more of these. To have a detailed understanding of plants' different needs, you need to differentiate between the different life cycles.

Woody Plants

The term "woody plants" refers to woody perennial plants such as trees and shrubs. It usually takes a few years for woody plants to become established and produce a significant cutting yield. They are best planted in locations where they can be at home for years and decades.

Trees

Trees characteristically form a leafy crown on a tall trunk. Trees can live for several decades to centuries. Fruit trees, whose flowering branches are used mainly in the spring, are particularly interesting for cut-flower cultivation. However, ornamental shrubs such as the ornamental cherry and trees whose foliage are used for greenery such as hornbeam or eucalyptus are also used in cut-flower cultivation.

Shrubs

Unlike trees, shrubs do not usually form a crown; their growth is basitonic (from the base). Shrubs also lignify, are perennial, and often live for several decades. Flowering shrubs are especially important for cut-flower production: beginning in early spring with the first blooms of fragrant snowball bush and forsythia to lilacs, roses, and hydrangeas. For me, shrubs are an important slow-flower building block. Dogwood and ninebark, for example, can be used for greenery. The fruits of the shrubs are also used—for example, I like to use rosehips or flowering quince.

Hedges

The term "hedge" describes a linear succession of several shrubby plants. In addition to pure production considerations, hedges can be planted for zoning large areas. They divide large spaces into smaller ones and can be used as privacy screens. In addition, hedges are natural wind breaks, can secure slopes with their roots, and provide a valuable habitat and food for hedgehogs, birds, snakes, and the like.

If you plant a few wild fruit plants such as elderberry, ornamental apple, juneberry, and sea buckthorn in your hedges, you will be rewarded with many four-legged and winged visitors within a year. In addition to enjoying a near-natural habitat, birds, hedgehogs, and other animals make themselves useful as natural pest control.

Perennials

Perennials are persistent, herbaceous plants that do not lignify. Their aboveground plant parts die over the winter, because they have a wide variety of overwintering organs such as rhizomes, bulbs, or tubers from which the plant sprouts again in the coming growing season. There are short-lived perennials that live only a few years, and very long-lived perennials such as the peony. The abundance of perennials that can be used as cut flowers is enormous, from daffodils and columbines to oregano, lavender, and chrysanthemums. All are perennials, and once grown in the location, terrific cut flowers can be harvested from them for years with minimal maintenance.

Biennial Seed Plants

Biennial seed plants describe plants that require two growing seasons from germination to seed formation. For cut flowers, biennial seed plants of interest include foxglove, sweet William, and evening primrose. Sowing in July and August with subsequent planting in the fall leads to flowering in the following spring.

Annual Seed Plants

The life cycle of annual plants takes place within one growing season. The germination of the seed, plant growth, flowering, seed maturation, and death of the plant—all this usually happens in the period from spring to the first autumn frost.

Rules are there to be broken. Systematics and theory are important for understanding relationships. But exceptions prove the rule! The distinctions described above were created by humans, and they do not influence nature. For example, snapdragons feel so comfortable in our greenhouse that they come back every year, even though they have not seeded.

SOIL

Soil Assessment

Next to the plant, garden soil is one of the most important garden resources. For successful gardening, it is essential to know your soil, to protect it, and to always strive to improve it! The first step is to get to know your own soil. This requires time and attention, and even a laboratory analysis cannot hurt. With a little experience, the first conclusions about the quality of soil can be made by examining it, especially in regard to its color and texture. A dark color may indicate a high humus content, which is good for plants because humus provides nutrients to the plant. In turn, a fine, crumbly soil is preferred by cut flowers over very sandy soil. In sandy soil, the nutrient-rich humus is washed out too quickly. In loamy soil, water and nutrients are well retained, but it is heavy and laborious to work by hand. Loamy soils can be loosened with the addition of humus or sand.

Soil Samples

But no matter how knowledgeable you are, I recommend taking a soil sample annually and having it analyzed in a laboratory; this will give you more clarity about the composition of your garden soil. After about two to three weeks, the lab results will provide information about the soil's consistency, nutrient levels, pH, and any existing pollutants. Most laboratories supplement their analyses with recommendations for soil improvement and organic fertilizers.

The Right Amount of Fertilizer

A well-known problem, not only in conventional agriculture but also in private and allotment gardens, is anthropogenic eutrophication or, in other words, man-made overfertilization. In the private sector, this usually happens because gardeners mean "too well" and fertilize too much. If the soil is already saturated with nutrients, the additional nitrogen and phosphates introduced with the fertilizer are washed out with the (rain)water and thus enter the groundwater and rivers and lakes. Too many nutrients in water bodies then lead to microbial-induced, increased oxygen consumption—rivers become algal, and lakes become biologically out of balance.

Therefore, I recommend taking a soil sample in the garden every year to check whether nutrients really need to be added to the soil before fertilizing.

Soil Protection through Green Manuring

In times of soil erosion—the loss of (top)soil through washouts and wind—it is important not to leave one's cleared beds fallow if possible.

I therefore urge all readers to become familiar with the subject of "green manure." On one hand, mulch layers can counteract erosion; more on this on page 37. On the other hand, targeted application of green manure, especially over the winter months, can protect soil organisms and improve soil structure. The idea behind green manuring is simple: various seeds are spread on beds that will not be used for a few months (or years). The plants that grow in the process are not harvested but die back on their own over the winter and are subsequently mulched or incorporated into the soil.

Some plants, such as white clover, increase the amount of nitrogen in the soil when sown as green manure, so it requires less fertilizing. However, this does not apply to all plants offered as green manures, so the term "green manure" is somewhat misleading. In the "Resources" section on page 215, there is a reference to a great organic seed supplier that has many different seeds for use as green manures (also known as cover crops) in their product line.

In my nursery, I use green manure in a strategic way, so I would like to briefly report on two examples. As soon as the first frost has passed over the dahlias in the fall, I dig up the tubers; this is described in detail on page 140. To prevent the soil from washing out in the winter, I have developed two strategies. When digging up the dahlias, there is always a lot of green waste: I use this as a layer of mulch on the beds. On the beds for which the dahlia mulch is insufficient, I sow hairy vetch or winter legumes. Once the seed has emerged, it prevents the soil from washing out and improves its structure. If it ever gets too cold and the green manure fails to germinate, I mulch the open beds with other greenery, tree, or hedge trimmings.

In May, after all the tulip beds are harvested, my tulip beds first need a break. I then seed a flowering strip mixture of marigold, crimson clover, sainfoin, and phacelia. As with all direct seeding, keep the soil moist for the green manure to germinate. Over the summer, great blooms develop that are loved by insects. In the fall, I then plant a new fall seeding. However, I don't plant any more tulips there for the time being.

Field Rotation

The location of a crop—for example, the aforementioned tulips—should rotate. From vegetable cultivation we know a very precise system of crop rotation that divides vegetable species into strong, medium, and weak growers. In (cut) flowers, I have not encountered such a subdivision. Nevertheless, rotation against soil depletion is a good idea. This is definitely true for crops such as tulips and dahlias. Many native flower species, such as cornflower, poppies, corncockle, and brown knapweed, can handle very lean soils and do not deplete the soil. However, if possible, I would also rotate these annuals and biennials. This is especially true if the crops have been severely affected by disease in the previous year. For example, I once had a rust (fungal disease) on cornflowers and snapdragons. As a result, I rotated the beds, and the next year the problem had gone away. Powdery mildew, downy mildew, and aphids, on the other hand, are not diseases that require field rotation for me.

LOCATIONS

Light Conditions

Light conditions in future flower beds are also important for a beautiful cut-flower garden. Most cut flowers do best in sunny locations. If you have a lot of sun in your garden, you will be lucky and have an abundant harvest.

However, many of the flower species are also fine with a partially shady spot, but they produce slightly fewer blooms there.

If you want to create a bed in the shade or your garden happens to be in the shade, choose your plants accordingly. I have some inspiration for shady beds from the Leipzig Riverside Forest. Its microclimate is always a bit darker, wetter, and cooler than in the city. Leather flower, ferns, masterwort, Japanese anemones, foxglove, French hydrangea, and climbing hydrangea cope well in this environment. Therefore, they can also be planted in spots that range from partial shade to shade in the garden. I can also recommend columbine, astilbe, ramsons, Christmas rose, wolf's bane, lady's mantles, hostas, lily of the valley, spring snowflake, coral bells, Solomon's seal, bleeding heart, bellflowers, and spurges. One advantage of the shady bed is that it usually requires less frequent watering. But beware: hungry slugs might feel especially at home in them!

Slugs

An important issue for many gardeners is hungry slugs. *Arion vulgaris*, incorrectly known as the Spanish slug, is a German-native slug species that has also migrated to North America and can cause great damage to agriculture and gardens. Most other slug species can be tolerated quite well in the garden, but be sure to check with your local garden center to determine if there are other species to look out for. For some years now, there has been talk of an explosive increase in *Arion vulgaris*. It is nocturnal, loves moisture, and loves to eat our young plants.

Their feeding marks can often be seen on the leaves. They eat the leaves from the outside in, usually leaving the leaf veins. A horde of *Arion vulgaris* can completely destroy a freshly germinated larkspur overnight. The small seedlings are then eaten away as if with a razor. Sometimes this leads to the false assumption that the seeds have not germinated, but it was the slugs that were faster.

Slug Prevention

I plant almost all crops as seedlings in the spring, so they have a chance against weeds and *Arion vulgaris* because slugs are not as fond of established plants. In addition, physical barriers can be used against slugs. There are slug fences for the entire bed, a slug collar for protecting individual plants, and copper strips that can be attached to the outside of raised beds and pots. Various materials are also recommended to prevent slugs. Suitable materials include shell grit, wood chips, coffee grounds, and sawdust.

Catching Slugs

I regularly catch *Arion vulgaris* myself at dusk because they are particularly active then. But you can also find them during the day under large leaves, stones, and wooden boards. There are also so-called collector plants; they include lettuce and comfrey. If the plants are planted selectively and kept somewhat moist in the evening, the unwanted visitors will gather there and can be caught easily. Beer traps are generally not recommended since they also attract slugs from surrounding areas.

Beneficial Animals to Prevent Slugs

An easy and ecologically valuable way to deter *Arion vulgaris* is to attract beneficial animals. Along with toads and hedgehogs, other slugs such as leopard slugs, Roman snails, and grove snails are natural predators. I would generally advise against the use of conventional slug pellets: they can also be harmful to beneficial animals, pets, and children. The so-called organic slug pellets consist of an iron-III-phosphate compound, which causes slugs to no longer be able to produce slime. Despite extensive research, I could not get clarification on whether other snail species, such as the Roman snail, are also affected or even killed by it. Therefore, I prefer not to use it.

GARDEN MANAGEMENT

Watering

Water is essential in the garden. The amount of water needed in addition to rainfall varies from year to year and from garden to garden. After planting, young plants, perennials, and woody plants always need a large portion of water; the "deep watering" helps them grow.

I use drip irrigation in my flower fields; more information is available on page 97. Drip irrigation was especially important in 2018 and 2019, which were particularly dry years. In contrast, I hardly needed it in the summer of 2020.

When watering, there are a few rules of thumb:
- To decide if you need to water, simply stick your finger about 4 inches (10 cm) into the soil and see if it's dry.
- It is best to get the water as close to the roots as possible to minimize water loss through evaporation.
- It's better to water a little more thoroughly but less frequently. This encourages the plants to develop a strong root system.
- Do not use a sprinkler in the heat of the day: the water droplets can burn the leaves when the sun is strong due to the magnifying glass effect.
- For those who have problems with slugs, water in the morning rather than in the evening. This allows the surface liquid to evaporate quickly, because slugs feel most comfortable in damp conditions.

Weeds

I have talked with many gardeners concerning weeds: their opinions and experiences were the same across the board. The most underestimated task for gardening newcomers is weed management!

All it takes is a heavy rain in April or May combined with three or four days of sunshine and warm temperatures, and the weeds get completely out of control! Direct seedlings don't stand a chance anymore because the seeds don't get light to germinate due to the fast-growing weeds. And freshly germinated or planted seedlings are overgrown by plants that are not supposed to grow in the bed.

Weeds are divided into seed weeds and perennial weeds. My personal challenges, if not my archenemies, are couch grass, field bindweed, thistle, and stinging nettle: the last two also because they sting and burn terribly. Unfortunately, I have not yet found a secret recipe against weeds. Spraying is out of the question, so a lot of manual work and good timing is required.

The first thing to do is to prepare the new beds well. I free the soil or the mulch layer from all unwanted plants. After that, it takes perseverance: from April to September, there is always the opportunity to weed. I usually remove perennial weeds by hand, which is the most effective way. Against unwanted emerging seeds, on the other hand, weekly hoeing between the rows helps.

It is also possible to apply layers of mulch, because the resulting lack of light hinders the germination of undesirable plants. For more on weeding, see page 80, and for more on mulch layers, see page 37.

Reseeding Timing

For advanced gardeners, the timing of reseeding is important. Many annual cut flowers have a main bloom phase. For example, snapdragons, which I love to use in summer bouquets, germinate within seven to fourteen days, and it takes 120 days to harvest the cut flower. For example, if you are very fond of snapdragons, cornflowers, or dill, you can sow a so-called reseeding every two to three weeks after the last sowing. Delayed germination results in delayed flowering: thus, you can harvest a species for months that would not flower other than for a period of a few weeks without reseeding. It is important to calculate so that the reseeded plants flower before the end of the season, which usually dates to the frost—otherwise the work would be in vain.

Then, starting in August, sow biennials and frost-tolerant annuals in what is called autumn seeding. More on this on page 136.

I love planning the garden and crops. I really enjoy taking time in the winter to do this. It feels a bit like four-dimensional Tetris in a way: advanced gardening.

Vacation

To end the topic of "garden management," I'd like to talk about taking vacation in conjunction with seeding timing. If you are planning a vacation of several weeks during the growing season, you should start looking early for a vacation replacement to water, monitor, and (if you are lucky) weed.

An important mindset here is the theme of "letting go," because even a week's vacation can be enough to make your own garden almost unrecognizable. You can mentally adjust to this and take it in stride.

For example, if you are planning a six-week summer vacation from early August to mid-September, you can consider during the prior winter whether you can move the sowing of annual flowers that bloom during this period up by sowing them early, or whether it would be better to do without them.

Long-Handled Tools

Tools should always be well cared for. For everything that comes in contact with soil, such as spades and hoes, a short cleaning after use is necessary. This is because in the long term, the humic acid in the soil affects the tools by making them rusty and dull.

LONG-HANDLED TOOLS

Left side (from left to right): lawn rake · hoe · cultivator rake · scuffle hoe

Center from top to bottom: Swedish hand weeder · vine shears · garden shears

Right side (from left to right): spade · shovel · Japanese garden knife · weeding trowel · brushes · garden fork

Hand Tools

As with the long-handled tools, a small, basic collection of hand tools is sufficient to maintain a garden, in my view. What is important is the regular maintenance of the tools. Everything that comes into contact with soil or sap should be washed or brushed off after use.

Hand Tools

Everything that has a blade should be sharpened regularly. For this, I use a whetstone. Then I oil the freshly sharpened tool.

From left to right: Swedish hand weeder · sickle · hand shovel · Japanese garden knife · dibber · garden shears · pruning shears · jute wire · brush · whetstone

Vases

All the vases pictured here are either from a flea market or were bought used online, or they originate from estate sales or long-forgotten storage in attics or basements. Only the white footed bowl, pictured in the middle, was bought "new" from a ceramicist friend.

Vases

These are my favorite vases and containers *(from left to right)*: Apothecary bottle · vintage vase · old milk bottle · small tulip-shaped jam jar · large canning jar · vintage jug · footed bowl · bottom part of a sugar bowl · brass bowl · silver-plated large footed bowl · small vintage vase

Materials

With my sustainable materials, I make sure either that they can be reused for many years, such as the vases and wreath bases, or that the materials are compostable in my garden.

Materials

For wrapping bouquets, I use 100% recycled paper. The flower paper can be recycled after use—see page 124. You can also use scrap newspaper.

From left to right: Metal wreath base · pruning shears · compostable jute wire *(below)* · paper tape *(middle)* · vase with two strips of tape · sticky wax · flower frog, large and small · natural raffia · chicken wire

Spring

Spring Essentials

- Prepare Soil and Beds
- Cultivation
- Divide Perennials
- Take Cuttings
- Planting

Spring Essentials

For me, spring is the most exciting time of the year in the garden. Starting in February, I begin to sow annual cool flowers and perennials, and starting in March, I sow frost-sensitive, annual summer flowers. Additionally, the beds are prepared for the upcoming planting. In the meantime, weeds are sprouting in all corners. But the most beautiful thing is when the first early bloomers appear in the flower beds, such as daffodils and irises.

PREPARE SOIL AND BEDS

Create Flower Beds

To start growing (cut) flowers, you don't need any more than a spot in the home garden, allotment, or balcony. There are several methods of preparing the soil for the upcoming garden year. Which method you choose depends on the size of the flower beds as well as the available time and manpower. The different methods can also be combined very well. Whether gardening is started within a few square feet or half an acre, the baseline situation should always be examined. In particular, this means the soil and light conditions.

Location Properties

I recommend taking an annual soil sample and having it analyzed in a laboratory. After about two to three weeks, the laboratory results will provide information about the condition of the soil, nutrient supply, pH, and any pollutants found. The light conditions of the future flower beds are just as important. Most cut flowers do best in sunny locations. Many of these flower species are also fine in a partially shady spot, but they usually produce fewer blooms there. If you want to create a bed in the shade, choose your plants accordingly. For example, ferns, Japanese anemones, hydrangea, and foxglove like it shady, a little more humid, and cooler.

Dimensions

For flower beds arranged in a linear fashion, it is recommended to plan at least 18 inches (45 cm) in width for paths. The beds should not exceed a width of 47 inches (120 cm) so that garden care can be done comfortably from the path.

Covering

If you find an area overgrown with grasses and have the time, I advise covering the beds and the paths with a UV-impermeable tarp or cardboard for several months. The light deprivation also suppresses perennial grasses, and after uncovering the soil is usually ready for planting. An added benefit is that covering protects the soil from soil erosion.

Prepare a False Seedbed

If there are many flying weeds in the area or if you assume that there are still active seeds in the soil, a false seedbed can be used to stimulate the weeds to germinate before planting. To do this, the prepared bed is kept damp to germinate a few weeks before the planting date. The best germination conditions for weeds are between 50°F (10°C) and 68°F (20°C). After about eight to ten days, the freshly germinated weeds can be removed by machine or hand (i.e., weeded, hoed, or dug up).

Build Mulch Layers

The mulch layers are built up in the first year by using cardboard and compost. The first step is to lay out unprinted carboard (important: no plastic adhesive tape!). This deprives the weeds below of daylight. The layers should overlap generously so that the grasses cannot find a way between the boxes. Now the box can be watered with a garden hose. This will make it even more attractive as food for earthworms and will withstand any upcoming wind. Next, apply a layer of 8–12 inches (20–30 cm) of compost. If your own compost is insufficient, pathogen-free compost can be purchased. Now the mulch layer is ready for planting or direct seeding. When planting, I use a Japanese garden knife or a dibbler (see page 24) and pierce through the cardboard once for the planting hole. This allows the plants to root through into the deeper soil more quickly. A major advantage of mulch layers, in addition to suppressing weeds, is that nutrients are returned to the soil. Furthermore, the mulch layer reduces water evaporation. In addition to compost, silage, straw, or wood chips can be used for mulching. I use wood chips only for shrubs. Depending on the composition of the wood chips and their age, additional organic nutrients may be necessary.

Digging, Tilling, and Plowing

When a large area needs to be made available quickly, tilling or plowing is usually done. This involves breaking up and turning over the soil with a motorized machine. If there is a lot of pressure coming from the root weeds, the roots often need to be removed from the bed in a further work step. If you are taking over an area that has already been agriculturally prepared, the soil is usually already dug up with a plow. Mechanical loosening of the soil has the advantage that you don't have to obtain and distribute large amounts of mulch material. However, deep plowing can disrupt soil organisms and capillaries and thus limit water storage capacities.

Rearrange an Existing Bed

If an existing bed needs to be rearranged and replanted, you can save yourself some effort. The discarded plants are moved or dug up and composted. This can be followed by a thin layer of compost, well-rotted horse or sheep manure, or an organic fertilizer, which can be applied and incorporated before planting.

CULTIVATION

Distribute Potting Soil

To begin, I fill a growing tray with moist potting soil. Potting soil is fairly easy to make yourself by mixing one-third garden soil, one-third compost, and one-third sand and sifting with a soil sieve if necessary. As an alternative to growing trays, small soil pots can be pressed, paper pots can be made with a paper press, or the seeds can be sown directly into pots.

Place the Seeds

Now, place one seed in each little pot. I store my seeds in a dry, cool, and dark place. Flower seeds are slower to lose their germination than, say, lettuce seeds, but each additional year of storage means a few percentage points less in germination rate. Your own seeds can also be used wonderfully for cultivation. The sowing time is usually written directly on the seed packets. Sowing times can be found in the bloom and harvest calendar.

Consider Greenhouse Light Conditions

Classically, we start sowing in the greenhouse. Plenty of light is essential to growing healthy seedlings. A sign of not enough light is long, unstable stems with few leaves. A windowsill may not be sufficient, and an additional light source should be used. For optimal plant growth, it is advisable to mix both cold and warm light sources.

About Light and Dark Germinators

When growing plants, a distinction is made between light and dark germinators. Most annual slow flowers are light germinators, which means that in cultivation they are covered with a maximum of half an inch (1 cm) of soil. Dark germinators include, for example, forget-me-nots, *Cynoglossum amabile*, annual and perennial larkspur, *Delphinium* sp., and nasturtium, *Tropaeolum majus*.

Dark germinators are covered with at least 1 inch (2 cm) of soil and do not need an artificial light source for germination. I place the dark seedlings under the greenhouse table for germination to have more space for the light germinators. In certain circumstances, the dark germinators can be additionally covered with a tray. After germination, the young plants as well as the light germinators need plenty of light to develop healthy and firm stems and leaves.

Cover the Seeds

Once all the seeds are in the pot, spread a thin layer of soil over them, and on top of that, a thin layer of sand. The sand serves a dual function. First, it prevents the top layer from drying out, and it also prevents the formation of mold.

Keep the Growing Tray Moist

Once the seeds are sown and covered with sand, I label the tray with a wooden sign and water it. The seeds need to be kept moist, because drying them out would interrupt the germination process. But be careful: conditions that are too moist can quickly lead to mold and root rot. Therefore, I recommend watering in moderation. Finally, cover it with a transparent hood and place it on the heating mat. Instructions for the construction of the heating mat can be found on page 188.

Fascinating Germination Process

The germination process usually takes between seven and twenty-five days. As soon as seedlings have developed the first cotyledons, the hood should be removed. The growing tray may then be removed from the heating mat and placed in a bright place. Even after many years, I am still fascinated every time little plants sprout from the small seeds.

DIVIDE PERENNIALS

Break Open the Root Ball
Most perennials can be propagated with cuttings or division. The chrysanthemum is carefully detached from its pot, and the root ball is broken open in the middle with your thumbs.

Separate the Perennial
When breaking up the root ball, I carefully pull apart the stems with the roots belonging to them. As the picture shows, one perennial forms up to eight plants, which can be planted individually after division. If the roots are connected, they can be cut with a knife in the middle between the small plants.

Planting
The isolated plants are placed in pots with fresh plant soil. It is important that the roots do not protrude upward and that they are completely covered with soil. The soil should cover the small plant at least as high as before, preferably a few centimeters higher.

Pressing the Soil

After placing the plants in the pots, I carefully press down the top of the soil. If necessary, I add a little more soil.

Rooting

After being divided, all the little plants are well watered. Over the next few weeks, the plants should be placed in a bright, airy place and watered sufficiently. Within a few weeks, the small plants will establish themselves in their pots.

Planting Out

As soon as the first white, thin roots are visible through the hole at the bottom of the pot, the plants are usually sufficiently rooted after a period of about six to ten weeks. Now they can be repotted or planted directly outdoors. Until the plants are established in their new location, they should be watered regularly.

Recommendation

For some plants, such as lavender or thyme, division every three to five years is rejuvenating for the plant. If they are not divided, the center of the plant becomes bare. By dividing your favorite perennials, the number of the plants in the garden can rapidly increase in a few years. In addition, a self-propagated plant makes a great souvenir or birthday gift.

However, beware—some varieties are subject to plant variety protection: this means certain plant varieties are considered intellectual property. If a plant variety is subject to plant variety protection, it may not be propagated and sold without the permission of the plant variety owner. This usually concerns commercial traders. It is advisable to read the latest legal texts; for example, at the Federal Office of Plant Varieties in Germany; you should contact the government office associated with agriculture in the country you are planting in, in order to be directed to the proper resources.

TAKE CUTTINGS

Gain Cuttings

Many perennials and woody plants can be propagated by cuttings. To do this, I use a sharp, clean knife to cut a shoot from the main plant at an angle about 2–4 inches (6–10 cm) above the soil. The lower leaves are removed from the cuttings to prevent rot and reduce the evaporation area. The slanted cut portion of the cutting is turned in cinnamon. This promotes root growth and prevents mold. The small cuttings are inserted into the soil to just below the first leaf base. The soil is then lightly pressed down around the small cutting.

Caring for Cuttings

All cuttings are watered and placed in a bright location. Lightly sprinkling the soil surface with cinnamon and regularly airing the cuttings with prevent fungal growth. A clear cover or jar placed overhead as well as regular moisture checks will keep cuttings from drying out during the first week.

PLANTING

Hardening Off Young Plants
Before I take young plants out of protected cultivation and put them into the open field, I let them harden off for several days. To do this, I put my growing tray with the young plants outside the greenhouse in a shady spot in the morning, then put them back in the evening. Important here as well: don't forget to water! The young plants can spend the last one or two nights completely outside before planting them out.

Putting Young Plants in the Ground
Planting is best done on a cloudy day or, if the weather forecast is sunny, in the morning or evening so that the sun does not put additional stress on the young plants. On planting day, I carefully push the seedlings out of the growing tray and gently break up the root balls with my hands. With a dibber, I shovel a small hollow in the soil in the prepared bed. The young plants —in the pictures, Chinese forget-me-nots are displayed—are partially placed into the hollow and gently pressed. The careful pressing of the small plants creates a small depression in the soil, which makes it easier for me to water later.

Watering Young Plants
Once all the seedlings have found their place in the flower bed, I water them heavily, creating a small puddle at each plant. The deep watering ensures that the roots can develop better in the soil. Finally, I align the irrigation hoses and set the irrigation.

Recommendation
I plant the flowers much more densely than is described on most planting guides, so that the leaf mass suppresses weeds, and the flowers form long stems. You can also plant under long-stemmed plants with ground covers. This has a similar effect against weeds.

Spring Garden DIY
===================

Spring Garden DIY

- Willow Tea

Spring Garden DIY

Willow tea serves as a natural rooting aid and growth regulator in the garden. I use it when taking cuttings and dividing perennials. Willow tea is best used in the spring. All types of willow can be used. Willow naturally contains salicylic acid and indole–3-butyric acid, which is used as a rooting hormone and growth regulator.

WILLOW TEA

- around 300 g willow branches
- around 1 liter warm water
- a container and a sieve

Prepare mixture

First, I cut young willow rods; here I use branches of corkscrew willow, which are no wider than your finger. It's not a problem if the leaves are already sprouting. I cut the rods with garden shears into pieces ¾–1 inch thick and pour warm water over them. Rainwater is best, but if only tap water is available, it should be left out standing for at least a day. Cold water can also be used optionally, but then the infusion should steep at least overnight.

Pour the Tea

I let the infusion sit for at least four hours and no more than a day, then pour it through a sieve. The remaining plant parts are then composted. To use, dilute the willow tea in a 1:2 ratio (one part tea and two parts water). I then water freshly harvested and planted cuttings with the dilution. For the next two weeks, the cuttings are watered with the willow tea infusion, using the same ratio, as needed.

Recommendation

In conventional horticulture, rooting powder is used as a growing aid. Since I couldn't find a natural product and didn't want to buy chemicals, I came across willow tea. Some sources recommend doing the infusion with warm water, some with cold water. I have had very good experiences with the infusion of warm water in the spring.

Spring Blooms

- Double Daffodil
- Apple Blossom
- Anemone
- Tulip
- Buttercup

Spring Blooms

From left to right: Sweet cherry (*Prunus avium*) · bird cherry (*Prunus padus*) · daffodil (*Narcissus* sp.) · guelder rose (*Viburnum opulus*) (horizontal) · apple blooms (*Malus domestica*) · tulips (*Tulipa gesneriana*, 'Foxy Foxtrott') · Persian buttercup (*Ranunculus asiaticus*, 'Champagne') · Tulips (*Tulipa gesneriana*, 'Columbus' and 'Blue Diamond') · Lenten rose (*Helleborus orientalis*, 'White Lady') · Persian lily (*Fritillaria persica*) · Persian buttercup (*Ranunculus asiaticus*, 'Purple Jean')

DOUBLE DAFFODILS
Narcissus 'Yellow Cheerfullness'

- **Location** Sunny to partially shady
- **Planting period** September to mid-December
- **Difficulty of care** Easy, self-propagating, resistant to snails, hares, deer, and voles
- **Plant type** Perennial
- **Bloom period** Mid-March to the end of April
- **Stem length** Up to 16 in. (40 cm)
- **Scent intensity** Medium to strong
- **Vase life** 7–10 days
- **Best harvest time** When the buds first show color

Special Characteristics:
- Daffodils reproduce through their bulbs. Every three to four years, the bulbs can be dug up and singled.
- To harvest the longest possible stalk, the flower stalk of the daffodil is "twisted out" by hand at the very bottom of the leaves.
- Daffodils secrete a milky liquid in the vase. This can affect other cut flowers.
- Therefore, daffodils should stand in a vase alone for at least thirty minutes after cutting and be put only in fresh water with other flowers after this liquid has been drawn out.
- Daffodils can be stored in the bud stage for up to three weeks in a cool, dark place. To do this, wrap a bunch of daffodils in newspaper, moisten the lower part, and keep the cut ends slightly moist.

APPLE BLOSSOMS
Malus domestica

- **Location** Sunny to partially shady
- **Planting period** September to mid-October
- **Difficulty of care** Once established, flowering shrubs are low maintenance, requiring pruning only once or twice a year for better yields
- **Plant type** Tree
- **Bloom period** March to June (depending on the woody plant)
- **Stem length** Depends on the size of the cut branch up to 24 in. (60 cm)
- **Scent intensity** Medium to strong
- **Vase life** Around 4–6 days
- **Best harvest time** When the buds first show color

Special Characteristics:

- Flowering branches can be cut from quite different woody plants.
- These include shrubs such as forsythia, lilac, snowball, juneberry, English dogwood, spireas, and weigela, as well as trees such as ornamental cherry, cherry, magnolia, pear, quince, flowering quince, apple, bird cherry, and flowering almond.
- When selecting woody plants, I pay particular attention to the bloom time, color, and fragrance. Depending on the planning and planting of the woody plants, flowering branches can be cut from January to the end of July.
- Cherry branches, forsythia, and snowball can be cut especially early, starting in December. As soon as the flowering branches are placed in water in a warm environment, they begin to bloom. In the past, the woody branch ends were broken open with a hammer. Today, this technique has been abandoned, but it is advisable to make the cut as large as possible. I use a good branch shears with which I cut the branches at an angle.
- After cutting, the branches should be placed in a vase immediately. The water in the vase should be changed daily, along with a new cut on the branch.
- After just a few days, the first petals begin to trickle down. I personally like this very much. Over time, more flowers bloom in the vase.

SPRING BLOOMS

ANEMONE
Anemone coronaria 'Pastel Galilée'

- **Location** Sunny to partially shady
- **Planting period** In autumn or early spring
- **Bloom period** March to May
- **Plant type** Perennial, but not winter hardy enough for our latitude
- **Stem length** 8–16 in. (20–40 cm)
- **Difficulty of care** Easy
- **Scent intensity Close to none**
- **Vase life** 7–10 days
- **Best harvest time** When the blooms are freshly opened

Special Characteristics:

- For planting, anemone tubers are soaked in water for about four hours. Then, they are placed in a planting home about 2–3 inches (5–7 cm) deep, with the tip up.
- If you plant in the fall, the location should be sheltered. Anemones are not particularly winter hardy and will freeze to death at temperatures below 14°F (–10°C). I plant my anemones in a greenhouse tunnel. At very low temperatures, the anemones are covered with an additional fleece, and in certain cases the tunnel is heated with candles.
- Anemone blooms can close again in the evening. You can recognize the best time for harvesting by the green cuff, which is located directly under the flower on the stem. Once the flowers are a little older, the stem grows so that the flower moves away from the cuff, marking the optimal time to harvest.

TULIP
Tulipa gesneriana 'Blue Diamond'

- **Location** Sunny to partially shady
- **Planting period** September to December
- **Difficulty of care** Easy, susceptible to voles and tulip fire
- **Plant type** Perennial
- **Bloom period** End of March to May
- **Stem length** 8–16 in. (20–40 cm)
- **Scent intensity** Middle to strong
- **Vase life** 7–10 days
- **Best harvest time** When the blooms first show color

Special Characteristics:
- Once planted, tulips usually bloom in the garden reliably for many years. However, if the tulips are harvested by cutting, sometimes the stem is cut so low that they cannot recover. That's why tulips used for cut flowers are usually planted fresh each autumn as an annual crop.
- If the tulips are to bloom the following year, a stem with at least two leaves should remain on the bulb.
- Harvested tulips can be stored in the refrigerator for two to three weeks. Either they are pulled out of the ground with the bulb and placed in the refrigerator dry, or the cut tulip is placed in water without the bulb. Then the tulips are stored in a cool place at 35.6°F–37.4°F (2°C–3°C).

BUTTERCUP
Ranunculus asiaticus 'Champagne'

- **Location** Sunny to partially shady
- **Planting period** In autumn or early spring
- **Difficulty of care** Demanding; not winter hardy; susceptible to aphids, blight, and root rot
- **Plant type** Perennial
- **Bloom period** End of March to May
- **Stem length** 12–16 in. (30–40 cm)
- **Scent intensity** Mild
- **Vase life** 7–10 days
- **Best harvest time** When the blooms are slightly opened

Special Characteristics:
- When planting, the buttercup rhizomes are soaked in water for about four hours.
- When planting in the fall, the location should be protected. Buttercups are not hardy and will freeze to death at temperatures below 23°F (–5°C). I plant my buttercups in a greenhouse tunnel. When the temperatures are very low, they are additionally covered with fleece and heated with candles if necessary.
- Buttercups are harvested as soon as the outermost petals start to protrude.
- Opened buttercups can also be dried.

Spring Floral Design

• Scented Arrangement

Starting in February, we can already harvest Christmas roses and blooming branches—the first cut flowers from our own garden. As soon as the bulb plants blossom in March and April, there is no flower wish that remains unfulfilled. In late spring, we can make arrangements with fragrant lilacs and colorful buttercups.

70

Spring Floral Design

- Spring flowers of your choice
- Clean bowl with base
- Chicken wire and wire cutters
- Fresh water and a pair of garden shears

SCENTED ARRANGEMENT

Preparation

In the first step, cut a piece chicken wire approximately 6 × 6 inches (15 × 15 cm) with a wire cutter. The chicken wire should be formed to a little ball and pressed in the bowl. It should sit securely and serve as an aid for inserting the flowers. Then the bowl should be filled with fresh water.

Set Corner Points

As a high point for the left side, I use the imperial crown: it is about twice as high as the footed bowl. I remove the leaves on the stems that would otherwise stand in water for all the plants. Your wonderful arch is then decorated with two stems of Solomon's seal, positioned slightly below. On the left side, angular artichoke leaves define the outermost corner, which lies offset at least one bowl width to the right. Both Solomon's seal as well as the artichoke leaves may protrude downward. In my floral design, the horizontal center is never the high point—I find these arrangements more exciting because the eye wanders among the flowers.

Strengthen Corner Points

In this arrangement, I put the focus on height on the left side and on width on the right side.

The left side is embellished with buttercup. Two buttercups close together reinforce the arch of the imperial crown. A buttercup positioned on the left edge of the bowl forms the first focal point facing forward. On the right side, a tulip forms the focus. The champagne buttercup defines the slightly offset "center" of the arrangement and should not be positioned too high.

Work in Focus: Flowers

I now work inward with about ten buttercups and two Christmas roses, starting from the strengthened corner points toward the center. I cut the stems boldly and short to give my arrangement compactness and density. If I feel that the corner points are weakened, I dress them up again with one or two flowers. That is the case here with the imperial crown.

Set Contrasts

With the help of the small, fragrant lilac flowers and the angular-shaped daffodils, I create a contrast to the round buttercup and tulip flowers and thus create depth in the arrangement. See my tips below for exactly how to cut lilacs and daffodils. Lilacs are a great flower for filling in gaps. It is important in this step to also design the back of the arrangement. The lilac is welcome to hang over the bowl. Now, when viewed from all sides, you should not be able to see any chicken wire. If there is, just fill it with a few flowers to hide it.

Mellow with Vases

I put four small vintage vases around the finished arrangement with single flowers and a golden bowl with a silk ribbon. I found the vases and bowl years ago at a flea market. Set this way, the still life is mellowed and can be placed on the dining table, the mantel, or the sideboard.

Recommendation

When daffodils are freshly cut, they should stand in a separate vase for at least thirty minutes. Daffodils secrete a liquid that can be toxic to other cut flowers and accelerate their aging process. Lilacs are best harvested early in the morning, when the upper flowers are still closed. Lilacs have trouble absorbing enough water in the vase, so I remove all the leaves on the stem. The next step is to make a cross-shaped incision in the lilac stem. To do this, I hold the lilac upside down and cut vertically into the stem with garden shears about ¾ inch (2 cm) and do the same thing after turning it another 90° so that there is a cross cut at the lowest part of the stem. In addition, it is important to give the arrangement fresh water daily!

75

Summer

Summer Essentials

- Weeding and Cleaning Out
- Fences, Netting, and Climbing Aids
- Fertilizing and Strengthening
- Cutting and Harvesting

Summer Essentials

Summer begins with the large peony harvest! The subtle smell of garden roses, sweet peas, garden cosmos, larkspur, and many other colorful cut flowers welcomes garden friends in the hottest time of the year. Along with harvesting and processing my flowers, I provide reliable water for the crops. Other summer jobs include plant care (i.e., pruning, fertilizing, strengthening, and support).

WEEDING AND CLEANING OUT

Weeding

"You can always weed!" is a common saying in my nursery. There is always a weed or grass growing somewhere that doesn't belong in the bed. I try to suppress many weeds and grasses with layers of mulch and very dense planting, but it still doesn't make my nursery completely weed-free.

Whether with a swing hoe, garden hoe, or Swedish hand weeder (*see photo*), or by hand, the goal is to remove the weeds along with all their roots when weeding. The tool used here depends on the type of plant and is also a matter of personal preference. I use swing hoes for row plantings and the Swedish hand weeder for fresh plantings and fall sowings, and I weed by hand in perennial beds, where the weeds grow very irregularly. After that, I leave the weeds, unless they are already forming seeds, right on the paths.

When talking to inexperienced gardeners, they are amazed at how much time is needed for weeding from March to October. My tip is to think of weeding as kind of a meditative process. Having your hands in the soil frees your mind and ensures a well-tended flower bed.

Pinching

To encourage branching of the plants, some flower species are pinched. This is where the topmost shoot tip is pinched with sharp gardens shears above the second or third pair of leaves. I recommend pinching for dahlia, garden cosmos, strawflowers, zinnia, and amaranth, among others.

Pruning

Pruning is a routine task in the flower garden in the summer. Faded flowers should be cut back regularly to keep the plants blooming. Once a plant goes into seed production, all the energy is put into this process. I prune dahlias, garden cosmos, and company at least once a week, using clean, sharp scissors to cut off the faded flower heads at the nearest branch fork. I leave the section on the paths and use it for mulching.

Some plants also need a little more rigorous pruning during the blooming season. Garden cosmos, roses, and dahlias in particular do well when long stems are cut for the vase. This creates a long and upright growth that forms new side shoots.

FENCES, NETTING, AND CLIMBING AIDS

A Fence for Dahlias

Dahlias need to be protected from the wind. This is done by fencing the freshly planted flowers. Bamboo poles are rammed into the ground every 2–3 yards. Around knee height, or at about 18 inches (45 cm), the first string is pulled once around the dahlia bed and attached to the bamboo sticks. The fence prevents strong gusts of winds from bending the plants. If necessary, the procedure can be repeated for larger plants at waist height.

Horizontal Nets

To protect crops such as garden cosmos from wind and weather, I let them grow through nets in our garden. I pull the nets across the ground right after planting. To do this, we ram bamboo sticks vertically into the soil. The net is stretched horizontally at knee height, about 18 inches (45 cm) above the ground, and fixed with wire, string, or cable ties. The plants will grow through the netting, and there is less risk them being damaged during strong winds in the summer or fall. If you do not want to use plastic nets, you can also use jute nets and compostable vine tie wire.

Climbing Aids

To support climbing plants such as sweet peas, morning glories, perennial vetches, and many others, you can either plant them directly against a fence or provide them with climbing aids. My sweet peas grow on a homemade trellis made of wooden stakes and vine-tying wire that is compostable every year.

For the basic setup, I ram a wooden stake about 3 yards long into the bed every 2–3 yards and connect the stakes horizontally with the wire. I start at the first stake by wrapping the wire around it twice and twisting the loose end in the opposite direction to the coil. Then I move on to the second stake and repeat the procedure, then to the third, and so on. At the last stake, I wrap the wire around it twice as usual, cut it with about 4 inches (10 cm) extra, and twist it around the stretch I just wound. I do another level every 8–12 inches (20–30 cm) in height and attach the horizontal wires to them. If the site is exposed to the wind without protection, the first and last stakes can be additionally braced with wire diagonally to the ground. I use hooks or pegs for this purpose.

There are countless ways to provide climbing aids. I especially like the idea of adding trellises to water tanks, disposal areas, and compost piles. There are also classics such as rose arches, ladders, or facades, which you often see lushly overgrown in allotments, backyards, or front gardens. There are no limits to the imagination here.

83

FERTILIZING AND STRENGTHENING

Fertilizing

I fertilize my cut flowers in the nursery only when necessary, and exclusively with organic fertilizers. In the flowering period, this can be once every six months or weekly. Crops and fertilizing methods differ from each other in this regard. All conditions must be considered: plant needs, available raw materials, and soil.

For example, I fertilize my dahlias during the blooming period from July to October every two weeks with nettle liquid manure, a versatile, short-term fertilizer. You can find out how to make it simply on page 94. White clover pellets are also suitable as a short-term fertilizer. On the other hand, my garden roses get a handful of sheep's wool every one and a half years, which I work into a small hole at the roots with additional nettle liquid manure from June to September every seven to ten days. Sheep wool is one of the effective slow-release fertilizers.

In addition to sheep wool, nettle manure, and white clover pellets, horse manure and sheep manure also make good organic fertilizers. These should be stored for at least a year, so that any grain that may be present does not cause unwanted plants to sprout. Some people also use slaughterhouse waste such as horn shavings. I have decided against it because my dog, Erna, likes to eat it. It is best to use fertilizer that can be made yourself or accessed locally, such as a horse stable in the neighborhood where you can inquire about it.

To determine whether the soil needs moderate or heavy fertilizer, I recommend having a soil sample analyzed in the laboratory. It is important not to blindly overfertilize the soil; otherwise, plant growth will be impaired, and nitrate, for example, can enter the groundwater.

Strengthening Plants

To protect against pests such as aphids or leaf fungi, there are different organic plant strengtheners, most of which can be made yourself. These are my favorites:

H2O SHOWER
- Effect: Fights against aphid infestations on my garden roses and dahlias without any pesticides.
- Application: I connect a watering attachment with a hard stream to the garden hose and spray the aphids off the plant daily for a period of about five to ten days.

LIVERWORT EXTRACT
- Effect: Helps with rust diseases and against powdery and downy mildew
- Application: Mix 5 ml of liverwort extract to 1 liter of water and apply every one to two weeks with a pump sprayer on the leaves. A manufacturer for liverwort extract can be found on page 216.

FIELD HORSETAIL TEA
- Effect: Helps against leaf fungi such as powdery mildew and rust.
- Application: Pour over 100 g fresh, crushed field horsetail with 1 liter of water and leave to infuse for at least one day. Then simmer for about thirty minutes. Sieve the plant parts after cooling. Apply tea on the leaves with a pump sprayer for three consecutive days.

GARLIC TEA
- Effect: Helps against leaf fungi such as powdery and downy mildew and should also keep voles away with its strong odor
- Application: Pour over one to two chopped garlic cloves with 1 liter of boiling water and leave to infuse for at least a day. Sieve the tea and dilute it with water in a 1:3 ratio. Apply to the leaves with the pump sprayer.

WHEY AND RAW MILK
- Effect: Helps against powdery mildew
- Application: Prepare a 1:1 solution with water and apply to the leaves with a pump sprayer. Spray the undersides of the leaves as well.

NETTLE LIQUID MANURE
- Effect: Helps with mild aphid infestations
- Application: See page 94

Compost tea and effective microorganisms also support leaf heath. I recommend delving further into the subject online or with the help of reference books.

CUTTING AND HARVESTING

Preparing the Harvest
In the early morning, when the fog still sits over the fields in the summer, the air is cool, and the meadow underfoot is still quite wet from dew, it's the best time to harvest flowers. I love the particular stillness that reigns on a cool summer morning in the city. I grab a sharp, clean knife and a freshly sharpened flower scissor and fill a clean bucket with cold water, and then it begins.

Almost every flower has its own individual window of time to make the perfect cut. In addition to the time window, the depth of the cut into the plant is also crucial. For many flowers, a good cut can promote the creation of new blossoms. Knowing about it secures your harvest success and preserves the pleasure of beautiful flowers.

In the Field
After cutting the flower, I remove the lower half of the leaves and loose branches while still in the field. I drop the green cuttings directly back onto the beds or paths, so they are allowed to mulch (i.e., decompose and form new biomass). My harvesting bucket filled with water is right near me in a shady spot. Immediately after cutting, I put the flowers in the water. If they are left in the air for more than two minutes, the conductive pathways of the stems dry out, and the cut flower can no longer optimally absorb water. In this case, I give them a fresh cut.

Each type of flower has an optimal harvesting stage, on one hand, to prevent them from "going limp" right there, and, on the other hand, to keep them as long as possible in the vase.

Dahlias
Jewel dahlias, ball dahlias, and giant flowered dahlias are best harvested when the flowers are fresh and fully bloomed. If harvested too early, the flowers may not open in the vase. Cutting too late can cause the petals to drop. Unfortunately, unflowered dahlias often have a very short shelf life in the vase.

Zinnias
Zinnias are quite different. They are harvested very late because the stalk does not harden until it has already been fertilized. I like to use the "wiggle test" by gently shaking the stem about 4 inches (10 cm) below the flower. If the head swings back and forth slightly, the flower is not yet ready for harvest and should remain in the field for two to three more days. If the stem is hard and stiff when I shake it, and the flower no longer swings, the zinnia is ready to harvest, and you are no longer in danger of snapping its too-young stem. Over the years, I have developed an eye for flowers, so the test is rarely necessary.

Wild Carrots and Company

Umbellifers such as wild carrot, dill, and khella should not be harvested too early; otherwise, they will quickly "go limp" in the vase. The best time is when the plant's first umbel is completely open. With wild carrot, dill, and khella, seed stalks are also attractive for bouquets and arrangements.

Sweet Pea and Co.

Many papilionaceous flowers, mints, and flowers in the buttercup family last much longer in the vase if they are already cut as soon as the lowest two to three flowers have bloomed. These include sweat pea, lupine, foxglove, and snapdragon, as well as annuals and perennial larkspur.

Garden Cosmos and Co.

Most composite flowers such as garden cosmos, sunflowers, and marigolds, but also shrubs such as roses, are ideally harvested before they have fully bloomed and been pollinated.

An example: In the picture below on the left, two garden cosmos can be seen. On the left in the picture, the flower is freshly opened, with the tubular flowers (yellow flower center) neither open nor pollinated. In comparison, the garden cosmos on the right in the picture has the tubular flowers already open, and the stamens with the black pistil are visible. The garden cosmos on the left will last at least five more days in a vase, while the one on the right may have already faded by evening and shed its petals.

The Exception of Poppy

In German, we use "poppy" to refer to different plant genera with different requirements. The genus *Eschscholzia*, for example, to which the California poppy and the gold poppy belong, is best harvested in a young flowering stage.

On the other hand, the genus *Papaver*, which includes opium poppies, corn poppies, and Iceland poppies, needs special treatment to last long in the vase. It is best to cut the flowers when the greens sepals are broken open, but the flower has not yet opened. After cutting, I dip the stem of the poppy in boiling water to a depth of 2–3 cm for about ten seconds and immediately place the plant in the vase with cold water. The boiling water causes the milky sap in the stems to coagulate, allowing for better absorption of the vase water. After that, the poppy should no longer be cut.

After the Harvest

I check each vase for absolute cleanliness before using it—if I don't want to drink from it, it's not clean enough for my slow flowers. To achieve a long vase life, it is also important to place the vase in a cool and shady place. Hot steam can cause premature blooming. I can take advantage of this by freshly cutting flowers that are too budded and placing them in (luke)warm water.

Summer Garden DIY

Summer Garden DIY

- Nettle Liquid Manure
- Drip Irrigation

Summer Garden DIY

In the hot summer months, everything revolves around good plant care and harvesting abundant flowers. For supplying them in hot weather, I use a drip irrigation system, whose construction is described on page 97. Additionally, I strengthen my flowers with a regular addition of nettle liquid manure: how it is prepared is described on page 94.

NETTLE LIQUID MANURE

- 2.2 lbs. (1 kg) nettles
- 2.6 gallons (10 liters) water (rainwater or stagnant tap water)
- A bucket (no metal!)
- A stick and a strainer
- Optional: marigold blooms

Homemade Fertilizer

Nettle liquid manure can be used to fertilize flowers and vegetables very inexpensively in your own garden. In addition, the misty liquid manure is excellent at protecting plant leaves from diseases and pests. One thing you need to know: liquid manure smells unpleasant, which is why the location should be considered. One summer, I had the nettle liquid manure set up right next to our outdoor seating area in the nursery. Depending on how the wind was, it was truly an intense olfactory experience at lunchtime.

Prepare the Mixture

Nettle liquid manure is best prepared in an airy place in the garden: as I mentioned before, it's a musty affair. To make it, chop the nettles and put them in a plastic bucket—you can add the optional marigolds here. The herbal mixture is then filled with 2.2 gallons (10 liters) of water. It should be stirred with a stick every day. After three weeks, the mixture is ready. A recommendation: Cover the top of the bucket with a fleece or net so that the air can escape, but insects cannot spread in it.

Spread the Liquid Manure

Before application, the nettle liquid manure is strained and diluted with water in a 1:10–1:20 ratio. The remaining liquid manure can stand covered for a few weeks. The sieved parts of the plant are disposed of in the compost.

The plants can be watered with the solution. Spreading the solution with a pump sprayer is even more effective. It is important to spray the leaves dripping wet on both the upper and lower surfaces. It is recommended to spray in the early morning or during the late evening hours in the summer. Nettle liquid manure can be applied as needed up to twice a month.

Recommendation: Good timing is important. If the plants are fertilized shortly before the harvest, the flowers will take on the odor. When vegetable gardening, fertilizer should not be applied several weeks before harvest, and even in organic gardening, please wash homegrown vegetables thoroughly.

Summer Garden DIY

- Hoses and small parts
- Irrigation computer
- Water connection

DRIP IRRIGATION

Drip Irrigation

As soon as a garden exceeds a certain size, an automatic irrigation system is indispensable. There are increasingly more hobby and allotment gardeners that use this kind of irrigation because it comes with many benefits. For one, the amount of water used is reduced because there is less that evaporates when watering. Also, the garden can be left alone for a few days during the summer without worry. There are regional differences here, so each gardener should definitely pay attention to the respective soil quality. A soil with heavy clay needs to be watered much less often than sandy soil. The same applies to shady locations and rainy summers.

In our nursery, we use timers—depending on their setting, the beds get watered once a day, dependent on the weather, for one to two hours. During longer periods of rain, we pause the watering, of course. A distribution hose goes off from the timers, which is connected to two to four drip hoses by means of a T-piece to distribute the water. Our drip hoses have a small hole every 12 inches (30 cm), from which approximately a third of a gallon (1.3 liters) of water escapes each hour.

The correct selection when it comes to the hoses

and timer depends on the available water source. If there are many spigots with high water pressure in the garden, you can also turn to professional equipment.

If you'd like, you can also connect the garden hose to your water source, kink the back end twice, and fix it with two cable ties. This way, no water escapes the end. But be careful: do not turn on the tap; otherwise the hose can burst from the pressure! Now, you can drill small holes on the underside at regular intervals of 12 inches (30 cm). A thin 1–2 mm diameter drill bit is well suited for this. Once a few holes are drilled, the water source can be carefully turned on. The holes spray a fine stream of water onto the ground. If your water source has low pressure, the amount of water can be controlled by the size of the holes. Automatic irrigation also must be regularly checked and maintained.

Connected systems can come loose and must be put back together. Hoses can become porous and punctured or even burst, and holes can become blocked with algae and lime and become clogged. Most hoses must be dismantled in the winter and stored in a frost-free environment. For me, however, the advantages clearly outweigh the disadvantages. Once installed in the spring, the automatic irrigation saves a lot of water and time.

Summer Blooms

Summer Blooms

- Peony
- Love-in-a-Mist
- Snapdragons
- Garden Cosmos
- Annual Larkspur

Summer Blooms

From left to right: Common hop (*Humulus lupulus*) (lying) · candle larkspur (*Delphinium elatum*) · zinnia (*Zinnia elatum*, 'Oklahoma Pink') · sweet scabious (*Scabiosa atropurpurea*, 'Black Knight') · wild carrot (*Daucus carota*) · panicled hydrangea (*Hydrangea paniculata*, 'Phantom') · Korean feather reed grass (*Achnatherum brachytrichum*) · dahlia (*Dahlia*, 'Fleurel') · garden cosmos (*Cosmea*) · garden rose (*Rosa*, 'Queen of Sweden') · dahlias (*Dahlia*, 'Princess Irene of Prussia') · basil (*Ocimum basilicum*, 'Red Rubin')

PEONY
Paeonia suffruticosa 'Inspecteur Lavergne'

- **Location** Sunny to partially shady
- **Planting period** In autumn
- **Bloom period** Mid-May to June
- **Plant type** Perennial shrub
- **Stem length** Up to 24 in. (60 cm)
- **Difficulty of care** Very low maintenance, little fertilizing, slug resistant
- **Scent intensity** Middle to strong
- **Vase life** 6–8 days
- **Best harvest time** In the so-called marshmallow stage—when the bud is about to blossom and yields to light pressure

Special Characteristics

- Peonies should be cut in the first years after planting only as an exception, because the plants need about three years to establish themselves in their location. The plants can live for several decades.
- Flowers cut at the marshmallow stage can be refrigerated for up to two weeks. As soon as the cut flower warms, it will bloom.
- Peonies should not be overfertilized, or they will become lazy in bloom. A single mild fertilization in the autumn is sufficient.
- The scent of bloomed peonies is dreamlike and unique.

103

LOVE-IN-A-MIST
Nigella damascena

- **Location** Sunny to partially shady
- **Planting period** Sowing under protection: starting mid-February, direct sowing is recommended.
- **Sowing** in open ground: autumn sowing in September or starting in mid-March.
- **Bloom period** June to September
- **Plant type** Annual
- **Stem length** Up to 24 in. (60 cm)
- **Difficulty of care** Easy to care for, can be propagated from own seed, slug resistant
- **Scent intensity** Weak
- **Vase life** 5–7 days
- **Best harvest time** When the flower has freshly bloomed or as a seed head

Special Characteristics

- I have had the best experiences when sowing love-in-a-mist in open ground in the autumn.
- They are best harvested directly after the blooms have opened. Cut buds also open in the vase.
- Love-in-a-mist bloom in a tender white, light blue, and shades of blue. New varieties are also available in pink and violet tones.
- The seed heads of love-in-a-mist are also easily cut. They can be used in fresh bouquets or hung up to dry.
- If you leave a few seed heads in the garden, love-in-a-mist will propagate itself.

105

SNAPDRAGONS
Antirrhinum majus

- **Location** Sunny to partially shady
- **Planting period** Sowing under protection: starting mid-January to March.
- **Sowing** in open ground: starting in March or at the end of August.
- **Bloom period** Mid-June to late October
- **Plant type** Annual, can be perennial in protected locations
- **Stem length** Up to 24 in. (60 cm)
- **Difficulty of care** Low maintenance, love warmth, can be propagated using own seed, slug resistant
- **Scent intensity** Weak
- **Vase life** 7–10 days
- **Best harvest time** When the lower flowers have freshly bloomed

Special Characteristics
- Snapdragons are harvested as soon as the lowest flower wreath has bloomed.
- The upper flowers open in the vase.
- Snapdragons have fine, edible blooms.
- Snapdragons bloom in a large variety of colors: from white to yellow, red, pink, and purple; striped with one or multiple colors; piebald to speckled.
- Routine pruning of the plant encourages flowering.
- Fertilization during the blooming period is recommended.
- Span a net over the plants directly after planting—this supports the snapdragons against strong winds in the summer. They can also be tied or staked.
- During mild winters or in protected locations, snapdragons can survive the winter.

GARDEN COSMOS
Cosmos bipinnatus

- **Location** Sunny to partially shady
- **Planting period** Sowing under protection: starting mid-March.
- **Sowing** in open ground: starting mid-May.
- **Bloom period** Early July to the first frost
- **Plant type** Annual
- **Stem length** Up to 48 in. (120 cm)
- **Difficulty of care** Low maintenance, love warmth, slug resistant
- **Scent intensity** Weak to middle
- **Vase life** 5–7 days
- **Best harvest time** When the flowers are freshly bloomed, and the yellow tubular flowers have not been fertilized yet.

Special Characteristics

- It is very important not to harvest garden cosmos too late, in order to ensure optional longevity in the vase. Like most composite plants, garden cosmos is harvested when the tubular flowers are closed and not yet pollinated.
- The (secondary) buds usually open in the vase as well.
- Garden cosmos flowers are edible.
- Regular deep pruning of the plant promotes flower formation.
- Fertilizing during the flowering period is recommended.
- The plants should be protected from strong winds starting in the summer at the latest. For this purpose, a net can be stretched over them directly after planting, or they can be tied and supported later.

ANNUAL LARKSPUR
Delphinium ajacis

- **Location** Sunny to partially shady
- **Planting period** Sowing in open ground: late August or starting in April.
- **Sowing** under protection: starting mid-February.
- **Bloom period** June to September
- **Plant type** Annual
- **Stem length** Up to 24 in. (60 cm)
- **Difficulty of care** Low maintenance, love warmth, can be propagated using own seed
- **Scent intensity** Weak
- **Vase life** About 7 days
- **Best harvest time** When the bottom flowers are freshly bloomed

Special Characteristics

- A direct sowing of the dark seedlings in autumn got me the best plants the following year.
- Larkspur is harvested as soon as the lowest wreath of flowers has bloomed. The upper flowers open in the vase.
- Both annual and perennial larkspur are poisonous.
- Regular pruning of the plant encourages flowering.
- Larkspur typically blooms in shades of blue. The variety of colors also ranges from white to pink to purple.
- Larkspur is very suitable as a dry flower; when harvesting, at least half of the flowers should be open.

113

Summer Floral Design

- Tying the bouquet
- Wrapping the bouquet

Summer Floral Design

The rich variety of summer garden flowers inspires my bouquets. Tying bouquets is a matter of practice—training to be a florist doesn't take several years for nothing. With patience and perseverance, you can learn this art on your own.

- Summer flowers
- Garden shears
- Natural raffia

TYING THE BOUQUET

Basics

The basic principle is that fine stems should not bend or break when tying, so that each flower in the vase is supplied with water. Additionally, there should not be any leaves in the vase water. The leaves would rot quickly and tremendously shorten the life of the cut flowers.

Clean Stems

Let's go! In the first step, I prepare my slow flowers and my cut greens for tying. For this, I clean the stems, which requires freeing the bottom half of the stems from leaves and branches.

Determine Corner Points

After all the stems have been cleaned, I determine the corner points of my natural summer bouquet. For this, I cross the two flower stems where the body of the flower begins, and move the flowers up and down until I have found my optional corner points for the bouquet.

Fill the Bouquet

In the next step, I always lay out the flowers from the top right to the bottom left. Here, it is important to always keep the same direction so that the stems do not bend each other. Admittedly, this step needs some practice to be done smoothly. In any case, it helps to decide on a feeder direction and then stick to it meticulously. Always from the top right to the bottom left, from the top right to the bottom left, and so on. As soon as twelve to fifteen stems have been worked into the bouquet, a spiral forms. Now at the latest is the time to check and see if a stem has accidently been worked in the wrong direction. The bouquet can now be turned in the hand so that flowers can be put in the bouquet from all angles.

Don't Forget the Fun

When tying flowers, keep calm and actively relax your hands, arms, and shoulders. You can have fun when tying flowers! With some practice, this special process can become a meditative practice. The attentive ordering of the flowers, forms, and scents gives me extraordinary pleasure.

Round Out the Composition

Among all the happiness that comes with the growing bouquet, I still take a critical look at it. Here and there I cut off leaves, stems, and blossoms. This is how an individual composition of leaves and flowers forms little by little.

Find the End

Now it is important to come to an end and finish up the process. People in my workshops and in other places have told me that this part is not always easy. Personally, I trust my intuition and encourage people to do the same. There is a clear point where I feel that the bouquet is finished. The golden rule is that a bouquet does not have to be perfect, but it needs to please. The gut decides this often better than the mind.

Tying the Bouquet

Now comes the tying. I lay a strip of natural raffia on the spot my hand was holding the bouquet (see the resources on page 214), and wrap it tightly two times around the bouquet. Afterward, I fix it with a double knot.

Most of the time, I wrap the rest of the raffia around the bouquet as well, because I like the thicker binding point. As I do this, I pay attention to pull the raffia tightly and fix it again with another double knot.

Anything left over is cut with scissors close to the knot. For me, it goes without saying that my bouquets are tied exclusively with natural materials. For one thing, I find natural raffia, linen, and cotton bands aesthetically very pleasing. In addition, it is just practical to be able to dispose of a withered bouquet, including the raffia, in the compost instead of fumbling the withered or even rotten stems out of the plastic.

Shorten the Stems

In the next step, all the stems are trimmed to one length. Additionally, I check if there really are no more leaves under the raffia.

Recommendation

After cutting, the finished bouquet is put in a vase filled with fresh water. The flowers should continue to be placed in a cool and shady location. I recommend cutting the bottoms of the stems, ideally daily, and putting them in a clean vase with fresh water. The summer bouquet can sit on the living-room table and bring life into the home or decorate a festive summer table. Now is the time to enjoy our natural summer bouquet with our own slow flowers!

Flowers as a Gift

Additionally, a self-tied bouquet is an ideal birthday present. If it is being made as a gift or has a long transport ahead, the bouquet needs to be wrapped. I will describe how to do this in the following pages.

One thing is for sure: a self-tied bouquet from your own garden delights both the recipient and the giver!

WRAPPING THE BOUQUET

- Recycling paper or newspaper
- Paper adhesive tape
- Sticker or greeting card if needed

Wrap the Bouquet

When I want to give my bouquet as a gift or transport it, I wrap it. This is uncomplicated and protects the delicate flowers.

In the first step, I fold the sheet of newspaper or recycled paper diagonally. I place the bouquet in the center of the folded sheet. The binding point, which is fixed with the natural raffia, is at the bottom fold of the sheet.

Now I fold the bouquet in from the left and right.

Using two strips of plastic-free tape and a sticker, I tape the sheet to the overlap and fold over one or two corners.

Autumn

Autumn Essentials

- Collect Seeds
- Autumn Sowing and Planting
- Dig Up and Store Dahlias

Autumn Essentials

In autumn, all garden lovers expect a richly filled sea of flowers. Along with dahlias, chrysanthemums, hydrangeas, larkspur, garden roses, wild carrots, and strawflowers also bloom. The autumn garden draws you in in its floral splendor, and it is time to tend the fields, harvest, and enjoy. I love to be out walking across the fields on a cool, foggy autumn morning and look up at the sky when I hear the wild geese on their way to their winter quarters.

COLLECT SEEDS

Use Open-Pollinated Seeds

The flowers you love don't have to be purchased new every year. Many annual slow flowers and even perennials can easily be propagated by using their own seeds for the next season. This saves money, and the plants that grow back are already well adapted to the site. To get the seeds, I stop cleaning out some of the plants during the summer. The bees and other insects do the rest. From late summer and into the autumn, you can then collect your own seeds.

If you want to collect seeds, you should use open-pollinated starting material. Open pollinated (OP) means that subsequent generations have the same characteristics as the mother plant and can be reliably propagated. OP seed is easily recognized by the fact that it is clearly labeled as such. I make sure that it comes from organic production as well.

Please note: If the seed is taken from special breeds with unusual colors, it may not be OP. Hybrid varieties are marked "F1." They cannot reproduce true to variety with the help of insect pollination. Should the plant produce seed, the offspring plants sometimes differ greatly in appearance from the mother plant.

Winning Your Own Seeds

Seeds are best collected on a dry afternoon. Mature seeds can be recognized by the fact that the seed coats are dry and no longer green, and the seeds have taken on a dark, black, or brownish color. Some seeds, such as nasturtium seeds, are beige brown when mature.

Dry, Clean, and Store Seeds

Once the seeds are collected, they should be well dried, preferably not in direct sunlight. The small seeds can be cleaned of plant debris by hand, with sieves, with a stream of air, or by blowing. The better dried and cleaned they are, the less chance there is of pests multiplying in them or mold forming. I store dried seeds in paper bags in a dark, dry, cool, frost-free place. Most flower seeds are able to germinate for several years. This is precisely why it is important to label the packets—after all, I want to know what I am putting in the ground later.

Natural Sowing

Many flowers sow themselves. For example, when the seeds of the love-in-a-mist fall on the ground, their offspring usually grow reliably the following year. This saves the steps mentioned above.

Recommendation

There are many types of flowers suitable for producing your own seeds, such as snapdragon, larkspur, love-in-a-mist, dill, amaranth, poppy, Iceland poppy, strawflower, coneflower, echinacea, garden cosmos, nasturtium, lupine, vetch, field bindweed, calendula, and wild carrot. Experimenters can try to take seeds from dahlias to breed a new variety.

AUTUMN SOWING AND PLANTING

Sowing Biennial Cut Flowers

I already begin growing the biennial cut flowers starting in July and August. Along with others, biennial slow flowers include foxgloves, sweet Williams, bellflowers, and annual honesty.

I sow the seeds in a growing tray and place it in the greenhouse or a shady spot outside. The important thing when sowing in the summer is not to forget to water! Then in September and October, I put the little plants in the ground so that they bloom next summer.

Sowing Annual Cut Flowers

Beginning in late August and continuing through September, many cold-tolerant annual slow flowers, also called "cool flowers," can be sown. For example, annual love-in-a-mist, field larkspur, Iceland poppy, snapdragon, cornflower, stocks, and Chinese forget-me-not are suitable for this purpose.

I usually put my annual autumn sowings in the ground without preplanting. To do this, I clear the designated bed of weeds, pull rows, and sow the seeds directly. The sowing is covered with a thin layer of soil and watered. A fleece to prevent water evaporation ensures that germination is not interrupted. The young and small plants are best overwintered in sheltered places. During the vegetation break, the leaf growth is slow. In return, the plants use the break to develop their roots.

The plants can also be sown in the spring. However, autumn sowing has some advantages that should not be underestimated. A stronger young plant usually develops after overwintering. In addition, autumn seeding scores points with its timing: I usually have time in the fall to prepare and seed a few beds. This takes the stress out of the large planting of summer annuals in the spring.

Last but not least, there are fewer slugs around in my nursery in the autumn to snack on the young plants, and there is less weed pressure.

In Leipzig, we have rather mild winters compared to the rest of the country. Autumn sowings here can be protected from heavy frost with a fleece. However, I do this only with the fragrant vetches.

Buttercups and Anemones

The large and elegant blooms of buttercups and anemones are among my spring favorites. I let both crops sprout in the autumn in planting trays filled with soil. Once the first pairs of leaves have developed, they are carefully planted in the greenhouse tunnel. The tender roots need a loosened soil to develop well.

Planting in the open is also possible in principle, but sensitive crops should be protected from heavy frosts during winter with a fleece. Anemones can survive a minimum temperature of 14°F (−10°C), while buttercups can survive temperatures down to 23°F (−5°C) without damage.

After planting in the greenhouse tunnel, anemones and buttercups should be carefully watered. Over the winter, they should be watered only as needed, and aired out regularly. Waterlogging, excessive soil moisture, and overly moist leaves are not liked by the two crops, since this puts them at risk of rotting.

In order to develop strong plants that produce many flowers, buttercups and anemone require a constant temperature of 50°F (10°C). As soon as the temperatures rise again in the spring, they reward us with their breathtaking beauty.

Woody Plants and Perennials

Autumn is the ideal time of year to plant most woody plants and perennials. The mild weather and regular supply of rainwater help plants develop robust roots. During winter dormancy, perennials and shrubs gather strength for the new year and have a head start over spring plantings.

Early Bloomers

Fall is also the time to cultivate early bloomers. For me, in September and October, many different kinds are put in the ground, such as tulips, daffodils, irises, ornamental garlic, crown imperials, hyacinths, crocuses, snowdrops, spring snowflakes, and others. Since the above species are perennial, I do not have to replant them every year, but only when a bed is newly planted or redesigned—or when the voles have eaten my bulbs in the summer again.

Many garden lovers know that early bloomers such as tulips make beautiful flowering accents in the beginning of the slow-flower year. It is worth mentioning here that the popular lily plants are grown as annual crops in traditional cut-flower production. Due to the hard cut in the spring, the bulbs do not have the opportunity to regain their strength and are no longer productive the following year.

Therefore, after the tulip harvest, the bulbs are usually composted. Meanwhile, there are more and more wild tulip bulbs available for purchase. Species such as vineyard tulips, Turkestan tulips, and Tarda tulips produce shorter stems but tend to go wild. In complete contrast to the tulip, daffodils and ornamental garlic species, for example, continue to grow after the flower harvest and propagate themselves.

DIG UP AND STORE DAHLIAS

Keep Track

After the first frost, dahlia tubers must be dug up and overwintered in a frost-free location. I strongly advise labeling the existing dahlia varieties before digging. After all, as soon as several tubers are unearthed, it becomes impossible to keep track of them, because despite the fact that the plants have different-colored flowers, the tubers hardly differ from each other. To better orient myself, I prepare several labels for each variety. I attach one label each to the main shoot near the ground. Another label is attached to the outside of the box in which the tubers spend the winter.

Digging the Tubers

Now the dahlia is cut back significantly just above the surface of the soil. Then I pierce the digging fork into the ground about 6–8 inches (15–20 cm) away from the main shoot. I highly recommend sturdy and heavy shoes for this! Then, I slightly lift the soil. With the digging fork, I poke once or twice in a circle around the tuber, being careful not to injure the part of the plant that's underground. Finesse is also required when levering the soil. Light levering motions loosen the soil, making it easier to pull the tuber out by the cut shoot. I then use a gentle shake to roughly remove excess soil and place the tuber in a box.

Wintering Conditions

I collect multiple tubers of the same variety in a box and then place it in a spot for overwintering. In this dark place, there should be a constant temperature between 41°F and 46°F (5°C–8°C). Once the tubers freeze, their only use is compost.

An essential influencing factor when storing dahlias is the humidity. If it's too high, the tubers can rot or mold. If the tubers are dug up during rainy days, I dry them for a few days in a warm spot. If the humidity is too low, the tubers shrivel. In this case, a bowl filled with water can help, which is placed next to the tubers.

Recommendation

I check my dahlias every one to two weeks during the winter in order to be sure that the storage conditions are continuously optimal.

Starting in late winter or in early spring, I clean out the storage area and split up my dahlias. There is more information on this on page 184.

Autumn Garden DIY

Autumn Garden DIY

- Drying Flowers

Autumn Garden DIY

The time for dried flowers already begins in summer and reaches its peak in autumn. Now is the right time to create a colorful store of flowers for the gray season. Dried flowers are great for bouquets and door and hair wreaths and can also be combined with fresh flowers.

DRYING FLOWERS

> - Fresh flowers, suitable for drying
> - Rubber bands
> - Clothesline

Harvest Dried Flowers

In contrast to your cut-flower harvest, dried flowers are best harvested during the heat of midday and late afternoon in sunny weather. The flowers should be matured and fully bloomed and the leaves of the flowers dry.

Drying Location

I rid the stems of my dried flowers of leaves and hang them in small bundles overhead on a clothesline. The drying location should ideally be airy, dry, and warm so that the bundles do not mold, and dark as well, so that the UV rays do not fade the colors.

If you prefer white dried flowers and a porous structure, you can let the dried flowers fade in the sunlight.

Store Dried Flowers

As soon as the flowers, seed stalks, and stems are no longer elastic, they can be taken down from the clothesline. They are best stored lying down or overhead.

In case the flowers have become too dried and fall apart easily, I lay them in the refrigerator for about a day. They gain a bit of moisture back in there, which helps significantly when working with them.

Preparation and Care

Dried flowers are most sustainable when processed untreated. Their shelf life is unlimited. If you wish, you can protect them from UV light and from crumbling apart with varnish or hair lacquer. If they are ever dusted, the flowers can be carefully puffed with a hairdryer.

Choice of Dried Flowers

Flowers for the budding harvest: strawflower, lavender, roses

Flowers for the mature harvest: paper daisy, ball dahlias, larkspur, yarrow, panicled and French hydrangea, silberdistel, safflower, buttercup, cockscomb, amaranth, everlastings, baby's breath

Seed stalks: poppy, love-in-a-mist, shepherd's purse, field pennycress, sorrel, various (meadow) grasses, cereals, hare's tail grass, reeds (please do not harvest wild), dill, amaranth, wild carrot, perennial honesty, (eagle) fern, physalis

Autumn Blooms

Autumn Blooms

- Garden Rose
- Dahlia
- Panicled Hydrangea
- Chrysanthemum

Autumn Blooms

From left to right: dahlia (*Dahlia*, 'Southern Belle') · strawflower (*Helichrysum bracteatum*) · dahlia (*Dahlia*, 'Myrtle's Folly') · brown-eyed Susan (*Rudbeckia tribola*) · basil (*Ocimum basilicum*, 'Red Rubin') · sunflower (*Helianthus annuus*) · rose (*Rosa*, 'Roald Dahl') · showy stonecrop (*Sedum spectabile*) · dahlia (*Dahlia*, 'Polka') · dahlia (*Dahlia*, 'Wine Eyed Jill') · wild carrot (*Daucus carota*) · cockscomb (*Celosia argentea*)

GARDEN ROSE
Rosa 'Roald Dahl'

- **Location** Sunny to partially shady and airy
- **Planting period** Autumn, sometimes in spring
- **Difficulty of care** Middle
- **Plant type** Perennial bush
- **Bloom period** June to the first frost
- **Stem length** 8–16 in. (20–40 cm)
- **Scent intensity** Middle to strong
- **Vase life** 5–7 days
- **Best harvest time** When the blooms begin to open

Special Characteristics

- Every garden rose should have about 11 ft.2 (1 m2) of space to prevent the formation of fungi on the leaves.
- In order to be able to cut roses as cut flowers as often as possible during the year, I recommend choosing frequently blooming rosebushes.
- In late winter, when the forsythias bloom, it's time to prune the roses. This is described in further detail on page 180.
- When planting, dig the hole deep enough so that the grafting location is below the soil surface. Adding mycorrhizal fungi to the planting hole will promote growth.
- Next to my rose beds, I planted herbs such as lavender, oregano, mint, and thyme. The herbs attract beneficial insects such as seven-spot ladybugs, which eat aphids. Moderate aphid infestations on roses can be tolerated in sustainable gardens because they can be kept in check by beneficial insects. However, if the infestation gets out of hand, the aphids can be sprayed off the rose with a garden hose for several days in a row.
- The roses are organically fertilized several times during the blooming period.
- Regular cleaning out of the faded parts of the plant prevents the formation of rosehips and encourages new blooms.
- Garden roses are best cut early in the morning, when the outermost petals begin to open. For the longest vase life, remove all but the top two leaves.
- The fragrance of garden roses, especially English cultivars, is unique. The nuances range from delicate and fruity, of lemon and apricot, to the intense and beguiling scent of the old rose varieties.

152

DAHLIA
Dahlia 'Peaches 'n' Cream'

- **Location** Sunny to partially shady
- **Planting period** After the so-called *Eisheiligen* (Ice Saints) feast days
- **Difficulty of care** Easy to care for, likes warmth, very sensitive to frost, can be propagated by dividing the root tubers
- **Plant type** Perennial
- **Bloom period** End of July to the first frost
- **Stem length** up to 32 in. (80 cm)
- **Scent intensity** Weak
- **Vase life** Average about 5 days
- **Best harvest time** When the flower is open, and the back petals are still intact

Special Characteristics

- There are thousands of varieties of dahlias. They are categorized into subgroups. These include, for example, large-flowering dahlias, decorative dahlias, waterlily dahlias, pompon or ball dahlias, and cactus dahlias.
- In spring, the root tubers can be divided; more on this on page 184. The tubers are planted about 4 inches (10 cm) deep in the soil after the so-called *Eisheiligen* (Ice Saints) feast days, usually around mid-May. Deep pinching of the plant at a size between 6 and 16 inches (15–40 cm) is recommended to encourage branching. Regular fertilizing during the blooming period can encourage flowering.
- It is best to protect the plants from strong winds starting in the summer, by using a fence, tying them down, or supporting them. The root tubers are dug up after the first frost and overwintered in a frost-free location, preferably at 41°F–46°F (5°C–8°C) in a dark room. Humidity should not be too high here so the tubers do not mold or rot.
- It is very important not to harvest the dahlia too budded; otherwise it will not continue to bloom in the vase.
- The (side) buds usually do not open in the vase.
- Unfilled dahlias and cactus dahlias often have a shorter vase life.
- Regular pruning of the plant promotes flower formation.

- **Location** Sunny to partially shady
- **Planting period** In the spring
- **Difficulty of care** Easy to care for
- **Plant type** Perennial shrub
- **Bloom period** August to October
- **Stem length** up to 12 in. (30 cm)
- **Scent intensity** Weak
- **Vase life** 10–14 days
- **Best harvest time** When all the blooms have opened

PANICLED HYDRANGEA
Hydrangea paniculata 'Phantom'

Special Characteristics

- Panicled hydrangeas are very easy to care for. Once grown in a location, they bring joy for decades.
- The shrub can grow up to 7–13 inches (2–4 m) high and should be planted with enough room to grow horizontally.
- The panicle hydrangea blooms on one-year-old wood. The flower color is initially creamy white and ages to shades of pink and red.
- The best time to harvest for the vase is when all the flowers are open to the top. If the flower is cut too early, it will wilt very quickly.
- For drying, the flower is best cut when the flowers begin to change color slightly in the autumn.
- Flowers left standing are a beautiful accent in the winter garden.

CHRYSANTHEMUM
Chrysanthemum x hortorum 'Julia'

> - **Location** Sunny to partially shady
> - **Planting period** In the spring
> - **Difficulty of care** Easy to care for
> - **Plant type** Perennial
> - **Bloom period** September to October
> - **Stem length** 16 in. (40 cm)
> - **Scent intensity** Weak
> - **Vase life** 10–14 days
> - **Best harvest time** When all the bloom is freshly opened

Special Characteristics

- Chrysanthemums, sometimes called mums, are the perfect finishing touch in the fall garden. Their colorful blossoms light the garden for months.
- When selecting varieties, it is important to pay attention to winter hardiness and longevity.
- Different varieties of chrysanthemums grow to different heights. I recommend choosing a medium height for cut flowers between 20 and 28 inches (50–70 cm).
- Chrysanthemums can be easily propagated by cuttings and division. Cuttings are described on page 45 and dividing perennials on page 42.

Autumn Floral Design

- Dried-Flower Wreath

A dried-flower wreath is the perfect way to enjoy the colors and variety of summer flowers during the gray winter. For the best results, the flowers should be thoroughly dried before tying; see page 146. In addition to flowers, I also use dried grasses and seed stalks. They give the wreath a wild character that I love.

- Dried flowers
- A metal wreath frame, diameter around 10 inches (25 cm)
- Around 3 yards of jute wire and natural raffia

DRIED-FLOWER WREATH

Create a Small Bouquet

After all the materials have been clearly laid out on a work surface, you can begin. First, I bind a small bouquet out of grasses, seed stalks, and dried flowers.

You can take your time for this step and release your creativity. Casual experimentation is desired when carefully combining colors and shapes together. I recommend using longer stems in the back and shorter ones in the front in the bouquet.

Tying the Bouquet

Now the dried flowers are tied by winding the ends of the jute wire around the stems and twisting them around each other. I wrap the bouquet about three times and then leave a little wire protruding. Afterward, the stems below the wire are cut so they are all one length.

Attach to the Hoop

Now the bouquet is attached to the hoop. For this, I tie the wire around the bouquet and the hoop at least three times. It takes a bit of skill to do this.

Just keep calm in case the bouquet loosens a bit—it can be brought back into shape and wrapped around once again to keep it in place.

Now I repeat the three previous steps to make a second bouquet. It is placed on the hoop in the opposite direction of the first bouquet. I then connect it to the hoop by wrapping all parts with wire. I shorten any protruding stems with garden shears. The wire should not be cut yet.

The Middle Section

The middle binding point still looks quite bare. This can be changed by putting a few blossoms on it and fixing them with the wire. In the end, you need a keen eye to examine the two bouquets and carefully align them to create a harmonious overall appearance.

Close Wire Ends

When all flowers are attached, I pull the beginning overhanging wire through a wire loop on the back of the wreath a few times. The wire end is cut with a wire cutter or a pair of pliers so that nothing else protrudes and no scratch marks can be left behind. Voilà—there is your finished wreath lying on your work surface!

Hanging the Wreath

The raffia is used to hang the wreath. I put it in a loop, which I tie with a simple knot, using both ends. This is how I fasten the wreath with a single loop: Pull the loop through the wreath, then pull the knot through the loop. With the knot in the raffia, you can vary the height of it as desired.

Recommendation

There are many diverse uses for leftover dried flowers; for example, for small bouquets, table decoration, or hair wreaths. They can be tied to a garland to decorate a room or set decorative accents as pin flowers on hats or jackets.

Winter

WINTER ESSENTIALS

Winter Essentials

- Overwintering Plants
- Planning Your Beds
- Rose Pruning

Time slows down in the garden during the winter. With the first strong frosts, most of the flowers go into hibernation, and time outside is limited for all garden lovers as well, due to low temperatures and limited daylight. I used to not like the cold and dark season. More recently, I have grown to appreciate the break for the plants, animals, and myself. The winter rest gives the garden a new aesthetic and gives me time to develop my new garden visions.

OVERWINTERING PLANTS

Winterizing

Even in the coldest season, I regularly visit my garden. With a hot cup of tea in my hand, I let my gaze wander over the snow-covered fields, breathe in the clear winter air, and enjoy the peace and quiet. Even now, I never get bored because there are always some little things to do. For example, the roses in the garden are heaped with compost to make them winter-proof; see page 180. The autumn sowings are hoed one last time and freed from unwanted weeds. Planted anemones and buttercups are also grateful to be weeded in the greenhouse tunnel, watered as needed, and protected from excessive cold.

In Extreme Cold

The frost protection chosen for the plants depends on the outside temperature. At temperatures below 23°F (−5°C), I use frost protection fleece for the anemones and buttercups in the greenhouse tunnel. It is placed loosely over the plants in the afternoon and remains there overnight. The next morning, or after a few days at the latest, I uncover the beds again to allow airflow to circulate around the plants.

If the temperatures ever drop below 14°F (−10°C), I use a homemade heater made of candles and clay pots, in addition to the fleece. Candles with long burning times are particularly suitable for this purpose. For this, candles are placed on the ground and lit, then I place a clay pot with a hole upside down over the candle.

The clay pots heat up slowly and reliably store the heat for several hours. Last winter, we had to fight temperatures as low as −4°F (−20°C) for many days. On those days, I placed ten to fifteen candles in our greenhouse tunnel, which has a usable area of about 375 ft.2 (35 m2). This saved the plants from damage from the extreme cold. When assembling, please make sure that the candles do not pose a fire hazard!

Overwintering in the Cold Greenhouse

I put my small collection of frost-sensitive potted plants such as oleanders, citrus fruits, geraniums, succulents, and proteas in the frost-free cold greenhouse before it starts to frost at night. It's light there, which is what they like. I water them about once a week. Once a week, I also check the stored dahlias. The frost-sensitive tubers are examined, and I remove moldy tubers if necessary. I also adjust the humidity when needed.

174

Prevent Frost Damage

Before we are free to go into hibernation, the water should be turned off and the water reservoirs should be emptied to avoid the risk of bursting and costly material damage. For me, this usually happens around St. Nicholas Day, December 6. By then at the latest, all irrigation computers and frost-sensitive parts of the drip irrigation system are dismantled, cleaned, and tidied up. Then it's time to fill the frost-free watering barrels in the greenhouse and foil tunnel. Afterward, all the outdoor pipes are closed and the water taps are turned on so that all the pipes are emptied.

Clear the Beds

Once the first frost indicates the end of the gardening season to us, it's time to get the beds ready for winter. We cover all the beds that were cleared by the end of October with vetch or green manure. On the remaining beds that have not been tidied, I leave the seed heads as feed for birds and wild animals. I also prepare a few corners with leaves as winter quarters for hedgehogs and other beneficial insects. The winter garden may seem lifeless at first glance, but in reality, some four-legged, winged, and crawling animals romp about here, where it offers shelter from the cold.

PLANNING YOUR BEDS

Develop Your Vision

I am always full of anticipation when I plan the beds for the coming garden year during the winter. I carefully calculate how many seedlings I need to fill my field, when they will be sown and hardened off, and where the seedlings will end up in the ground. I have made myself a bed plan on a scale of 1:250 as an essential basis for this, on which my more than fifty beds are marked. All perennial crops such as shrubs as well as the original tree population of the nursery are also shown on it. For the beds of annual crops, blank areas have been entered for the time being. So, I can copy the plan every year and fill it according to my wishes and visions for the upcoming season—that motivates me a lot!

When brainstorming ideas, on the one hand, I go back to an overview of the crops from the previous year that will be planted again. On the other hand, I have kept a wish list throughout the year of species and varieties I would like to try. I get inspiration for this during my visits to other gardens and flower farmers around the world.

The big puzzle begins. Equipped with my bed plan and my ideas, I start to fill the empty beds with a pencil. There are few things to consider. For example, crop rotation makes sense when planting dahlias and tulips. Sometimes a bed change is also necessary; for example, if the crop was plagued by disease the previous year. And sometimes the bed provides a home for the same crop over several years. For me, this includes love-in-a-mist and the Chinese forget-me-not.

These species propagate themselves so well that once established, they manage almost without my intervention. But whatever you want to grow in your own garden, you just have to try it out. Be brave!

Organize Seeds

I store the weeds of annual and perennial flower species in boxes in a cool and dry place. It is basically divided into annuals and perennials there. The number of boxes depends on the size of your seed stock. I now have five cartons full of seeds.

Each box contains a seed category such as "annual flower species" and is divided into individual compartments sorted in alphabetical order. I use the first letter of the botanical names because they are more distinctive than the German names. For example, the marigold *Calendula officinalis* is assigned to the annual flower species box and is sorted in compartment "C" for *Calendula*.

Recommendation

You can use any system you like! The primary thing is that it allows you to easily find the seeds you are looking for. Seeds should be used as soon as possible, and on the basis of my experience, I know that we flower lovers tend to buy a lot and then forget which inventory we stored from the previous year. What really counts is to keep an overview.

Order Missing Planting Material

After planning and inspecting your inventory, the orders for the coming season are placed. A good orientation for this is provided by the list of species and varieties that I am missing for the coming season. Because not everyone starts with such a list, I have my recommendations for seeds, perennials, shrubs, etc. in the back of the book in the "Resources" section; see page 214. New slow-flower farmers especially may be overwhelmed by the range of colors and shapes of ornamental plants that are offered, and there is a danger of getting lost in catalogs and websites. So, I keep calm and allow myself to get inspired by seed suppliers, but at the same time I try to stay true to my planning. When I spontaneously fall in love with a species, I look in the bed planning to see where it could have a place, and I may have to replace another one with it. And in the next season, all the cards are reshuffled. Order quantities are also quite difficult to estimate at the beginning. Do I get 5 g of this and that type of seed, or a thousand kernels? Here it is crucial to consider the size of the bed and the planting distances. If you want to grow cut flowers, you can plant most crops a little closer together; see page 48. I usually add 10%–20% more seeds to allow for the germination rate as well as failures in growing and planting. This is how I end up with a realistic order quantity.

ROSE PRUNING

Earthing Up Roses

Since ancient times, the rose has been regarded as the "queen of flowers" and among amateur gardeners as an extremely demanding plant. Many a person has gritted their teeth over it. However, there are only a few basic rules to follow in order to enjoy the flowers, which have been praised for thousands of years, and their enchanting fragrance for a long time.

In early winter, usually late November or early December, I earth up each of my shrub roses with two to three shovels of compost. The compost layer protects the grafting site from severe cold.

Pruning Roses

Pruning roses is usually done during the very last weeks of winter. An old rule among gardeners is that roses are cut back when the forsythia are in bloom. I would like to follow that with another message: pruning roses is less complicated than some may fear. Rambler and climbing roses are pruned less often, if at all, so I recommend rose pruning for rose shrubs. This requires high-quality, sharp pruning shears.

In the first step, I cut back shoots that are long and hanging to the ground. Then I shorten the entire plant by about a third, so that it develops a compact shrub shape. If the rose was planted within the last two years, the pruning is a little sparser. Now I thin out the center of the bushes. This improves air circulation in the summer and reduces the risk of leaf diseases. I then remove any shoots that look dead or diseased, as well as all foliage and the fruit (rosehips).

Pruning Debris

What happens to the foliage and the removed stems after pruning is a matter of opinion. As long as there are no signs of fungal infestation, I see no reason why they should not be composted. Top rose growers, on the other hand, consistently recommend disposing them with the regular waste. If possible, I would burn the cuttings. This will most certainly render the fungal spores harmless, and the ashes can be returned to the garden cycle via the compost.

Winter Garden DIY

- Divide Dahlia Tubers
- Build a Heating Mat

Along with the cleaning and repairing of my tools, I have time to improve my garden equipment for the coming season. The cold season is wonderful for building a heating mat for the upcoming cultivation in the spring and for dividing dahlia tubers.

DIVIDE DAHLIA TUBERS

- Undivided dahlia tubers
- Spray hose for washing
- Sharp garden shears

The Dahlias

Dahlias are perennial but are sensitive to cold at the same time. Therefore, it is essential for their survival that they are dug up in the autumn and stored frost-free throughout the winter; see page 140. In the spring, the root tubers can be divided with garden shears. On the one hand, this stimulates plant growth, and on the other hand, about seven to eight offspring can be produced from each mother plant. The divided tubers are also easier to plant than the unsplit, unwieldy tuber.

Preparation

First, I wash the soil from the tubers with a spray hose and remove the thin roots to get a better impression of the condition of the tuber and an overview of the places for division. Each tuber must have at least a thickening, a (slightly thinner) neck, and an eye (the point of budding of the tuber), so that a dahlia plant can grow from it.

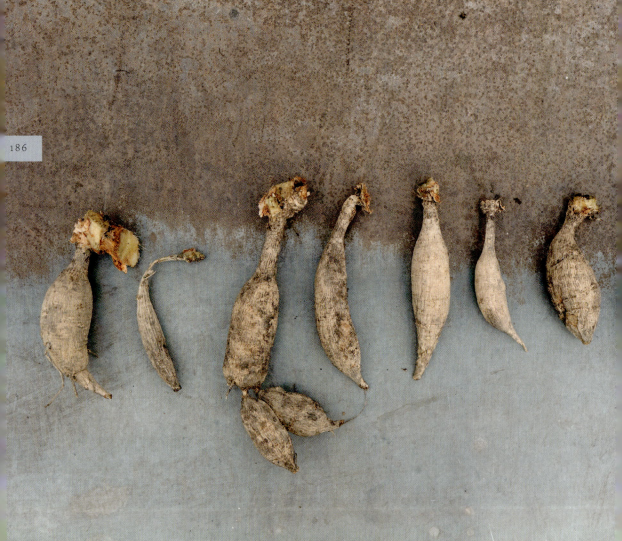

For dividing, I recommend very sharp and pointy garden shears. With it, I divide the tuber in the middle first. With very large, awkwardly shaped, or stubborn tubers, I also carefully use a hand ax for the first spilt.

Divide Tubers

Now I section off tuber by tuber, always with the neck and eye. This is how one undivided tuber can create several divided tubers—in the last picture above, there are about eight. After the so-called *Eisheiligen* (Ice Saints) feast days, the divided tubers can then be planted individually in the ground in order to please us with their unique flowering splendor from June into the autumn.

Sharpen Tools

If there is sand or dirt in the spaces between the tubers, the garden shears will quickly become blunt. If necessary, I sharpen the tools in between when cutting dahlias. To do this, I clean the plant residue from the garden shears with a little warm water and dish soap and then dry them. After that, I rub the cut surface with the grindstone and then oil the moving parts of the shears afterward.

BUILD A HEATING MAT

- A pond-heating cable
- Self-adhesive aluminum foil
- Painter's tape
- A thermostat with temperature sensor

Do it Yourself

Heating mats are often high priced in retail stores. However, if you still have a desire to start growing in an unheated greenhouse, you can quickly and inexpensively build a heating mat yourself with only a few components: the following instructions have been developed by my colleague Arjen Huese.

Mark the Area

I use painter's tape to mark an area on a large table or the floor that is 55 × 40 inches (140 × 100 cm). Depending on your needs, the size can vary. I then make more markings along the short side every 8 inches (10 cm). They help orient me later when I am laying the cable paths.

Lay Out Heating Cable

Now I add my pond-heating cable. I use a 40-foot (12 m) heating cable with 150 watts of power. It is waterproof and rated IP68, so it won't be hazardous when watering. The heating cable is laid out straight with a 4-inch (10 cm) gap from the edge of the 55-inch (140 cm) side. This is the first of a total of seven strips. After that, I lead the heating cable back in a round arc with a distance of 4 inches (10 cm) parallel to the first track. I orient myself on the taped markings. This creates the second track, and so it continues until all seven tracks are on the surface.

Adhering the Cable with Aluminum Foil

Now apply several strips of self-adhesive aluminum foil next to each other and—importantly—overlapping on the entire surface with the laid-out cable. The foil should protrude 4 inches (10 cm) at the outer edges. When the laid-out cable is completely covered with foil, the cables are lightly pressed. After that, the entire construction is turned over so that the foil is at the bottom, the adhesive side is facing up, and the cable is already adhered to it. In the next step, I lay several strips of self-adhesive foil overlapping and closing off the edges, just like on the back. Finally, everything is carefully smoothed.

Recommendation

I put a reusable sheet of Styrofoam between the heating mat and my plant table. Connecting a thermostat with a temperature sensor between the heating cable and the socket is recommended. Depending on the desired germination temperature, the thermostat can be programmed. I put the sensor directly into the soil of the growing tray and usually program the thermostat between 64°F and 72°F (18°C–22°C).

Winter Blooms

- Amaryllis
- Flowering Cabbage
- Christmas Rose

Winter Blooms

From left to right: rose (*Rosa*, 'Roald Dahl') · eagle fern (*Pteridium aquilinum*) · rosehips (*Rosa multiflora*) · mistletoe (*Viscum album*) · milk thistle (*Silybum marianum*) · panicled hydrangea (*Hydrangea paniculata*) · ornamental apple (*Malus*) · amaryllis (*Amaryllis*, 'Minerva' and 'Pink Rival') · blue spruce (*Picea pungens*) · flowering cabbage (*Brassica oleracea*) · white cedar (*Thuja occidentalis*) · annual honesty (*Lunaria annua*)

AMARYLLIS
Minerva 'Pink Rival'

- **Location** Light, between 68°F and 77°F (20°C–25°C)
- **Planting period** September to December; the bulb needs about ten weeks from potting to flowering
- **Bloom period** Mid-November to the end of April
- **Plant type** Perennial, bulb
- **Stem length** 24–40 in. (60–100 cm)
- **Difficulty of care** Easy in the first year, significantly more difficult after
- **Scent intensity** Weak
- **Vase life** Around 10–20 days
- **Best harvest time** When the first blooms have opened

Special Characteristics

- Amaryllis likes to be placed in a warm and bright place.
- They bloom in the winter and are special eye-catchers if they are grown between 68°F and 77°F (20°C–25°C). In the cold greenhouse, they bloom in the spring. Amaryllis is not frost hardy.
- If you want to see your amaryllis bloom again during subsequent years, fertilize the plant once it starts to flower. The amaryllis bulb needs an eight-to-ten-week break starting in July to bloom again. For this, the plant is cut back, and the bulb is stored in a cool and dark place. After the rest, the bulb is planted in a pot with fresh potting soil and watered just a little until the first new shoots appear. In this way, the bulb will continue to bloom in future years between November and March.
- Not enough humidity—for example, because of a fireplace—shortens the vase life of the amaryllis.
- The long flower stems are hollow on the inside, which allows you to be able to hang it as an installation upside down and fill it with water.

FLOWERING CABBAGE
Brassica oleracea

- **Location** Light, between 68°F and 77°F (20°C–25°C)
- **Planting period** Sowed under protection: May to June
- **Sowed** outdoors: May to July
- **Harvest time** Mid-August to January
- **Plant type** Annual
- **Stem length** Up to 24 in. (60 cm)
- **Difficulty of care** Difficult because cabbage attracts many different pests
- **Scent intensity** Weak, like cabbage
- **Vase life** around 14–21 days
- **Best harvest time** After the first frost

Special Characteristics

- Flowering cabbage is planted out about three months before the first frost (normally around the middle of October).
- Cabbage usually requires a cultivation protection net against pests such as the cabbage butterfly. As soon as the winter cold has set in, the net can be taken off.
- Cool temperatures create interesting leaf colors.
- Flowering cabbage is harvested before it blooms. As a decorative element, the leaves are arranged in a round shape, reminiscent of a flower.
- Flowering cabbage smells slightly of cabbage—a dash of vinegar or lemon juice in the vase reduces odor development.
- I like to leave some of the flowering cabbage in the beds in the winter and harvest them very late. This way, I still have a few stems from my outdoor cultivation in January.

CHRISTMAS ROSE
Helleborus x orientalis 'White Lady', 'Pink Lady'

- **Location** Partially shady
- **Planting period** Ideally from September to November, also possible in the spring
- **Blooming time** Mid-December to April
- **Plant type** Perennial shrub
- **Stem length** 6–18 in. (15–45 cm)
- **Difficulty of care** Easy, moderate nutrient requirements (fertilize twice a year), low danger of pests, can self-propagate
- **Scent intensity** Weak
- **Vase life** around 7–15 days
- **Best harvest time** Very late when the flower is already forming seeds

Special Characteristics

- Christmas roses bloom during the winter. For me, they are especially important as cut flowers because they develop strong white, pink, and dark-red blooms during a time where there is hardly anything available to harvest outside.
- They are harvested very late. I make sure that the first seeds in the inner flowers can already be recognized.
- If the Christmas rose is harvested too early, it can already start to wilt after just a few hours in the vase.
- When dealing with an early harvest, the flower stems can be scored after harvesting so that the water can be better absorbed. For this, you use a sharp knife to score along about two-thirds of the length of the stem. This should be repeated multiple times for each stem, then put the stems in water for twenty-four hours.

Winter Floral Design

- Festive Centerpiece

Winter Floral Design

Just because it's gray and dreary outside doesn't mean that we have to do without lush greenery and bright blossoms. For centuries, especially during Advent, people have been bringing winter arrangements into their homes. I also make a festive table bouquet each year before Christmas Eve, which charms the family well into January.

FESTIVE CENTERPIECE

- A brass tub
- Chicken wire and three flower frogs
- Conifer greens and blue spruce
- Dried fern
- Rosehips and ornamental apples
- Amaryllis and the last garden roses
- Flowering cabbage
- Dried orange slices, pine cones, and nuts

Prepare Insertion Mechanism

First, I place three flower frogs in the clean brass tray. Then I add chicken wire in the form of a cylinder or an egg. I bend the wire so that it fills the tub as completely as possible just below the rim. I then pour water into the tub until it is about two-thirds full.

Create the Green Base

I create a strong, green base for my arrangement, using two conifer species. To do this, shorten the individual branches of the tree of life and remove the scale-shaped leaves from the lower third so that they are not in the vase water. The branches may extend well beyond the tub and should cover the mechanisms such as the chicken wire or the flower frogs from the side. The blue spruce adds another dimension to the base with its cool-blue hue and spiky texture.

Dried Treasures

Now I use the dried fern as a golden ornamental element. My slow-flower friend Anne Oberwalleney calls dried flowers, seed stalks, and grasses "lovely dead crap"—and I think it fits perfectly! After the ferns, I use rosehip sprigs to echo the curved fern leaves. Ferns and rosehips are allowed to extend well beyond the sides of the tub and are also welcome to hang over the front.

Set Flower Accents

Afterward, I stick four amaryllis stems into the tub. The frog flowers we inserted in the beginning ensure stability. The stems are shortened to a fitting length and are carefully stuck through the chicken wire to the flower frog. In my design, I leave the middle of the arrangement free of flower accents and work toward the sides in a higher and more expansive way.

Add Flowers

The arrangement gets even more charm when more blossoms and leaves are inserted. Therefore, I work in three to five stems of garden roses and three to five stems of flowering cabbage. I group the flowers around the amaryllis flower accents. This creates a harmonious overall picture.

Insert Materials

Finally, I add three ornamental apple branches. The little apples hang over the tub. A few dried hydrangea flowers are put into the remaining gaps. It doesn't matter if the hydrangea heads were cut short, because dried flowers do not need to reach the water supply. A handful of cones, nuts, and dried orange slices loosely distributed on the table round off the festive arrangement perfectly. I water my bouquet about every two days so that the tub is always at least two-thirds full of water. Now Christmas can arrive!

The Authors

Chantal Remmert, a landscape architect and cofounder of the slow-flower movement, works under the name Erna Primula—Flower Studio and has been growing slow flowers in Leipzig since 2018.

Grit Hartung works and lives as a photographer in Leipzig. Since 2019, she has specialized in documentary photography and accompanies families and companies in this capacity.

We were brought together through a workshop in Chantal's nursery. Grit was taking pictures of the workshop, and it was immediately clear to us that we wanted to pursue common paths both professionally and privately.

Acknowledgments

We worked on this book for just under two years, including conception, photo and text production, and layout. During this process, we experienced numerous ups and downs: the book project pushed us, gave us hope, and gave us courage.

We would like to express our special thanks to Dr. Martin Lind and the team at the Haupt Verlag in Bern. They believed in our idea and always energetically supported us. Many thanks to Arjen Huese for the instructions for building the heating mat. Thanks to Martha Lothringer, Ulla Gerber, Peggy Giertz, Anne Oberwalleney, Sabine Panster, Julia Zitzelsberger, and Clemens Breitweg for your support and constructive criticism.

Many thanks to our families who always supported us—and not just during this crazy project. And thanks to our model "Erna," who always wanted to participate in the photo shoots: well rested, cheerful, and full of enthusiasm.

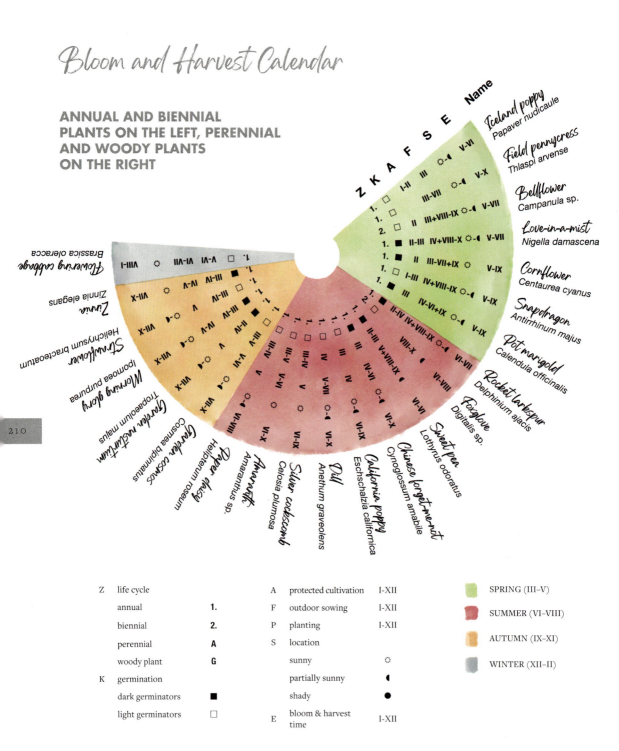

Bloom and Harvest Calendar

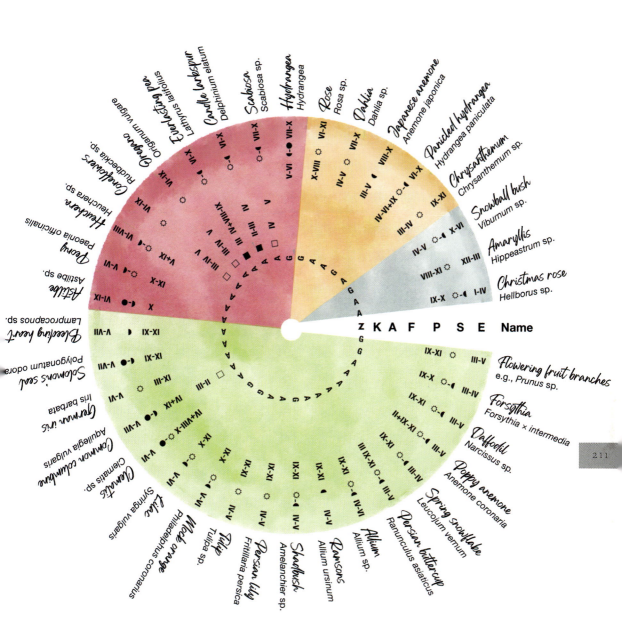

Garden Work Calendar

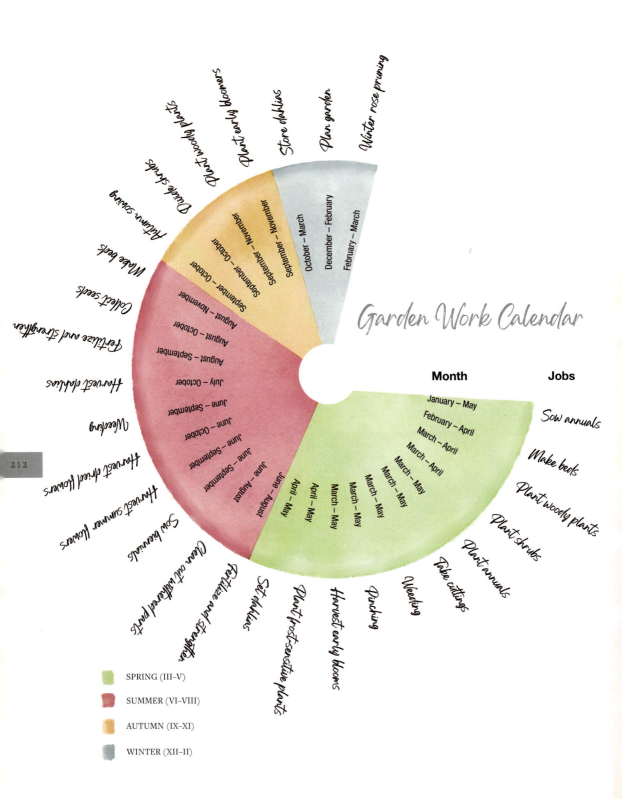

213

Resources

FURTHER EDUCATION

BOOKS
ENGLISH-LANGUAGE LITERATURE
    Ingrid Carozzi: *Ingrid's Vintage Flowers*
    Erin Benzakein: *Cut Flower Garten: A Year in Flowers*
    Susan McLeary: *The Art of Wearable Flowers*
    Ariella Chezar: *The Flower Workshop*
    Lisa Mason Ziegler: *Cool Flowers*

GERMAN-LANGUAGE LITERATURE
    Magrit De Colle: *Bio-Schnittblumen aus dem eigenen Garten*
    Bex Partridge: *Everlastings How to Grow, Harvest and Create with Dried Flowers*

    GENERAL GARDENING
    Karin Schlieber: *Prinzip Permakultur*
    Carolin Engwert: *Abenteuer Garten*

ONLINE RESOURCES, BLOGS, AND WORKSHOPS
ENGLISH LANGUAGE
    Floret Flower Farm: *www.floretflowers.com*
    Ponderosa and Thyme: *www.ponderosaclassroom.vhx.tv*
    Lisa Mason Ziegler: *www.thegardenersworkshop.com*
    American Horticulture Society Resources: *www.ahsgardening.org/gardening-resources*

GERMAN LANGUAGE
    Aus Dem Garten: *www.aus-dem-garten.de*
    Hauptstadtgarten: *www.hauptstadtgarten.de*
    Slow-flower movement: *www.slowflower-bewegung.de*
    Fördergemeinschaft ökologische Zier- & Gartenpflanzen (FÖGA)
        (website currently under construction): *www.bio-zierpflanzen.de*

Shopping

INTERNATIONAL SEEDS
Johnny's Selected Seeds (USA), assortment partially certified organic: *www.johnnyseeds.com*
Floret Flower Farm (USA): *www.floretflowers.com*
Geo Seed (USA): *www.geoseed.com*
Baker Creek Heirloom Seeds (USA): *www.rareseeds.com*
Bingenheimer Saatgut AG (Germany), certified organic: *www.bingenheimersaatgut.de*
Dreschflegel Saatgut (Germany), certified organic: *www.dreschflegel-saatgut.de*
Jelitto Staudensamen (Germany), assortment partially certified organic: *www.jelitto.com*
Erna Primula Blumen & Saatgut (Germany): *www.erna-primula.de/produkte*
Chiltern Seeds (UK): *www.chilternseeds.co.uk*
Muller bloemzaden (Netherlands): *www.mullerseeds.de*

PERENNIALS AND WOODY PLANTS
Gilbert H Wild & Son (USA): *www.gilberthwild.com*
Prairie Moon Nursery (USA): *www.prairiemoon.com*
Heirloom Roses (USA), also sells a wide variety of bulbs: *www.heirloomroses.com*
Mountain Valley Growers (USA): *www.mountainvalleygrowers.com*
Eden Brothers (USA): *www.edenbrothers.com*
AllgäuStauden (Germany), certified organic: *www.allgaeustauden.de*
GartELL (Germany), certified organic: *www.gartell.de*
Staudengärtnerei Gaissmayer (Germany), partially certified organic: *www.gaissmayer.de*
Bioland Hof Jeebel (Germany), certified organic: *www.biogartenversand.de*
David Austin Roses (UK): *www.davidaustinroses.com*
Native Plant Finder (native plant inspiration by zip code): *https://nativeplantfinder.nwf.org*

EARLY BLOOMERS
Brent and Becky's Bulbs (USA): *www.brentandbeckysbulbs.com*
Old House Gardens Heirloom Bulbs (USA): *www.oldhousegardens.com*
Tulip World (USA): *www.tulipworld.com*
Ecobulbs 't Keerpunt (Netherlands), certified organic: *www.ecobulbs.nl*
JUB Holland (Netherlands), certified organic: *www.jubholland.nl*

RECOMMENDATION: Seeds and planting material from abroad are subject to customs and import regulations. Current import regulations should be checked in advance especially when ordering from outside one's home country. Speak to your local garden center to find local sources.

MATERIALS

Adhesive wax at Shor International: *www.ishor.com/sticky-wax*
Vine-binding wire and paper tape at Felt Paper Scissors (USA): *www.feltpaperscissors.com*
Tinctures and plant extracts at Hawaii Pharm (USA): *www.hawaiipharm.com*

You can also find these materials, as well as chicken wire, raffia, plant strengthening materials, flower frogs, jam and preserving jars, and wreath bases, at your local hardware store or by shopping online. Etsy, Amazon, and eBay can also be useful sources for the specific materials mentioned in this book.

HORTICULTURE NEEDS

A.M. Leonard (USA): *www.amleo.com*
Gardener's Supply (USA): *www.gardeners.com*
Hermann Meyer (Germany): *www.meyer-shop.com*
GEM Gärtnereinkauf Münchingen (Germany): *www.gem-bedarf.de*

At these venues, at your local garden supply center, or by browsing online, you can find drip irrigation systems, potting soil, garden tools, and much more.

Garden soil and compost can be purchased locally at the soil or disposal plant, or at your local hardware or garden supply store.

NOTE: For seeds, planting materials, and horticultural supplies, there are companies that have specialized in either private or corporate customers. Some serve both customer segments. The locations listed above have been selected for inspiration. Contact your local garden center or reputable online resources such as the American Horticultural Society for further guidance in identifying gardening resources, clubs, or organizations.

All links valid and directing to active websites at the time of publication.

Index

A

Achnatherum brachytrichum 101
amaryllis 191, 192
anemone 63, 136, 139
Anemone coronaria, 'Pastel Galilee' 63
annual honesty 191
annual larkspur 13, 110, 136
annual seed plants 15, 136
Antirrhinum majus 107
apple 60
Arion vulgaris 18
arrangement 71
autumn sowing 136

B

basil 101, 149
bed planning 176
bed preparation 34
beneficial animals 19
biennial seed plants 15, 136
blue spruce 191
botany 14
bouquet tying 117
    wrapping 124
Brassica oleracea 191, 195
brown-eyed Susan 149
buttercup 67, 72, 136, 139

C

California poppy 90
candle larkspur 101
carrots, wild 90, 101, 149
celosia 149
centerpiece, festive 202
Christmas rose 72, 197
chrysanthemum 13, 15, 131, 156
Chrysanthemum × *hortorum*, 'Julia' 156
cleaning out 80
climate 12
climbing support 82
cold 172
cold greenhouse 172
columbine 15
cornflower 136
corn poppies 90
Cosmea bipinnatus 109
covering (beds) 34
cutting 88
cuttings, taking 46

D

daffodil
    double 58
dahlia
    digging up 140
    dividing tubers 184
    storing 140
dark germinators 41
Daucus carota 101, 149
deep watering 48
Delphinium ajacis 110
Delphinium elatum 101
design, floral 68, 114, 158, 200
digging 37
dogwood 14
dried flowers 145, 156
    wreath out of 161
drip irrigation 97
drying flowers 146

E

eagle fern 191
early bloomers 139
elderberry 15
eucalyptus 14
evening primrose 15

F

fences 82
fertilizing 85
festive centerpiece 202
field horsetail tea 85
floral design 68, 114, 158, 200
flower bed creation 34
flowering cabbage 13, 191, 195
flowering quince 14
forsythia 14
foxglove 15
frost 13, 172
frost damage avoidance 175

G

garden cosmos 13, 80, 90, 101, 109
garden management 20
garden rose 13, 101, 131, 150
garlic tea 85
geography 12
greenhouse 175
    light conditions 41
green manure 16
growing trays 41

H

H$_2$O shower 87
hand tools 24
handle tools (*see* long-handled tools)
hardening off (seedlings) 48
harvesting 88
heating-mat construction 188
hedges 15
Helianthus annus 149
Helleborus × orientalis 197
hornbeam 14
humus 16
hydrangea 14, 131
Hydrangea paniculata, 'Phantom' 101, 155, 191

I

Iceland poppy 36, 90

J

juneberry 15

K

Korean feather reed grass

L

larkspur, annual 13, 110, 131
    candle 101
lavender 15
light conditions 18
    in greenhouse 41
light germinators 41
lilac 14, 72
liverwort extract 85
location 18
    characteristics 34
long-handled tools 22
love-in-a-mist 13, 104, 136
Lunaria annua 191

M

Malus domesticus 60
materials 28
measuring (beds) 34
microclimate 12
milk thistle 181
mistletoe, white berries 191
mulching 36

Index

N

Narcissus, 'Yellow Cheerfulness' 58
nets 82
nettle liquid manure 85, 94
Nigella damascene 104
ninebark 14
nitrogen 16

O

Ocimum basilicum 101, 149
open-pollinated seeds 132
oregano 15
ornamental apple 191
ornamental cherry 14
overwintering (plants) 172

P

panicled hydrangea 101, 155, 191
peony 102
perennials 15, 139
    separating 42
phosphate 16
Picea pugens 191
planting (seedlings) 48
planting trays 136
plowing 36
poppy 90
    California 90
potting soil 37

R

Ranunculus asiaticus, 'Champagne' 67, 72
raw milk 85
reseeding, timing of 21
resources 210
Rosa multiflora 191
Rosa, 'Roald Dahl' 150, 191
rosehip 14, 191
roses 80
    pruning 180
Rudbeckia triloba 149

S

scabious 101
Scabiosa atropurpurea, 'Black Knight' 101
sea buckthorn 15
seasons 12
seed
    cleaning 132
    collecting 132
    drying 132
    open-pollinated 132
    organization 176
    placement 38
storage 132
suppliers 17
seed plants, annual 15, 136
    biennial 15, 136
shrubs 14
Silybum marianum 191
slugs 18
snail collection 19
    prevention 18
snapdragons 107, 136
snowball bush 14
soil 16
    organisms 17
    preparation of 34
    protection 16
    sample 16, 34
sowing 135
stocks 136
stonecrop 149
strawflower 131
strengthening (plants) 85, 87
sunflower 149
sweet pea 82, 90
sweet William 15

Index

T

Thuja occidentalis 191
timing of the reseeding 21
tree of life 191
trees 34
tulip 64, 72
Tulipa gesneriana, 'Blue Diamond' 64, 72

V

vacation 21
vase 26, 72, 90
Viscum album 191
vision development (for bed planning) 176

W

watering 20
weather 12, 82
weather app 12
weeding 80
weeds 20, 80
whey 85
wild carrots 90, 101, 131, 149
willow tea 54
winterizing 172
woody plants 14, 139
wreath of dried flowers 161

Z

zinnia 13, 88, 101

Note

All information in this book has been carefully researched, checked, and tested and reflects the current state of knowledge at the time of the book's publication. However, knowledge as well as laws regarding plant cultivation continue to develop and change, and new discoveries are added. Therefore, I would like to ask each reader to check whether the respective findings are outdated or not. This especially is relevant in regard to plant strengthening and biological fertilizers: here I recommend reading the included instructions carefully and using products accordingly. Furthermore, all of the information in this book was written in reference to German regulations, and the regulations may differ widely in different countries, so it is important to check with your local authorities: calling your government agency associated with agriculture is a good place to start.

Plant growth and flowering times are influenced by climate factors. The flowering and harvesting times given in the book are approximate values that can be transferred to your own garden and adjusted if necessary. Speak to your local garden center about applying these practices to your local climate zone.